TOILET TRAINING is one of the most challenging—and most rewarding—processes parents face. Based on the latest research and recommendations from the American Academy of Pediatrics, this essential handbook answers common questions parents have about toilet training and bedwetting, including:

- How will I know when my child is ready to be toilet-trained?
- What do I do if my child resists?
- How can I handle bedwetting and other accidents?
- What's the best way to encourage progress in my child?
- What do I do if my child is constipated?
- How do I choose a potty chair for my child?
- What kind of positive reaction should I have if my child has accidents?
- Should I potty train my toddler before he enters preschool?
- How should episodes of bedwetting be handled?
- How long does the toilet-training process take?

. . . and much more, to ensure a positive and enriching experience for both parents and children as they face this important developmental milestone.

Additional Parenting Books from the
American Academy of Pediatrics

**COMMON CONDITIONS**

ADHD: What Every Parent Needs to Know

Allergies and Asthma: What Every Parent Needs to Know

The Big Book of Symptoms: A-Z Guide to Your Child's Health

My Child Is Sick! Expert Advice for Managing Common
Illnesses and Injuries

Sleep: What Every Parent Needs to Know

Waking Up Dry: A Guide to Help Children
Overcome Bedwetting

**DEVELOPMENTAL, BEHAVIORAL,
AND PSYCHOSOCIAL INFORMATION**

Autism Spectrum Disorders:
What Every Parent Needs to Know

CyberSafe: Protecting and Empowering Kids
in the Digital World of Texting, Gaming, and Social Media

Mama Doc Medicine: Finding Calm and Confidence
in Parenting, Child Health, and Work-Life Balance

Mental Health, Naturally: The Family Guide to Holistic Care
for a Healthy Mind and Body

**NEWBORNS, INFANTS, AND TODDLERS**

Baby Care Anywhere: A Quick Guide to Parenting On the Go

Caring for Your Baby and Young Child: Birth to Age 5

Dad to Dad: Parenting Like a Pro

Heading Home with Your Newborn: From Birth to Reality

For additional parenting resources, visit the HealthyChildren
bookstore at shop.aap.org/for-parents/.

*This book is also available in Spanish.

American Academy of Pediatrics
# GUIDE TO TOILET TRAINING

AMERICAN ACADEMY OF PEDIATRICS

# GUIDE TO
# TOILET TRAINING

Second Edition

## MARK L. WOLRAICH,
## MD, FAAP,
## EDITOR-IN-CHIEF

BANTAM BOOKS
NEW YORK

# REVIEWERS AND CONTRIBUTORS

EDITOR-IN-CHIEF
Mark L. Wolraich, MD, FAAP

AAP BOARD OF DIRECTORS REVIEWER
David Bromberg, MD, FAAP

AMERICAN ACADEMY OF PEDIATRICS

CEO/EXECUTIVE DIRECTOR
Karen Remley, MD, MBA, MPH, FAAP

ASSOCIATE EXECUTIVE DIRECTOR
Roger F. Suchyta, MD, FAAP

DIRECTOR, DEPARTMENT OF PUBLISHING
Mark T. Grimes

MANAGER, CONSUMER PUBLISHING
Kathryn Sparks

EDITOR
Holly Kaminski

DIRECTOR, DEPARTMENT OF MARKETING & SALES
Mary Lou White

REVIEWERS & CONTRIBUTORS
Paul F. Austin, MD, FAAP
Amanda Berry, CRNP

Nerissa S. Bauer, MD, MPH, FAAP
Nathan J. Blum, MD, FAAP
Timothy Brei, MD, FAAP
Timothy Bukowski, MD, FAAP
Michael Carr, MD, PhD, FAAP
Edward Christophersen, PhD, FAAP
George Cohen, MD, FAAP
Beth Ellen Davis, MD, MPH, FAAP
Beth DelConte, MD, FAAP
Edward Goldson, MD, FAAP
Damon Korb, MD, FAAP
Irene McAleer, MD, FAAP
Lane S. Palmer, MD, FAAP
Peter J. Smith, MD, FAAP

FIRST EDITION REVIEWERS & CONTRIBUTORS
F. Daniel Armstrong, PhD
George C. Cohen, MD, FAAP
William L. Coleman, MD, FAAP
Barbara J. Howard, MD, FAAP
J. Lane Tanner, MD, FAAP
Hyman C. Tolmas, MD, FAAP

WRITER
Richard Trubo

ILLUSTRATIONS BY
Anthony Alex LeTourneau

This book is dedicated to all the people who recognize that children are our greatest inspiration in the present and our greatest hope for the future, and to Seneca and Eleanor, who managed to toilet-train themselves before being able to benefit from this book's advice.

Mark L. Wolraich, MD, FAAP

# PLEASE NOTE

# CONTENTS

# FOREWORD

The American Academy of Pediatrics (AAP) welcomes you to the second edition of *Guide to Toilet Training*.

Helping a child through the toilet-training process can be one of the toughest challenges for parents. Although learning to use the toilet independently is a natural part of growing up, parents often wonder: "How do I know when my child is ready?" This book will help parents learn how to recognize the physiological, cognitive, and verbal signs that indicate when a child is ready to toilet-train. Many other important topics are also addressed in this book, including how to deal with accidents and regressions, toilet-training an older child or one with special needs, and navigating through bedwetting and soiling episodes.

What separates *Guide to Toilet Training* from many others in bookstores and on library shelves is that it has been developed and extensively reviewed by physician members of the American Academy of Pediatrics. Because medical information is constantly changing, every effort has been made to ensure that this book contains the most up-to-date findings. Readers may want to visit the official AAP website for parents at www.HealthyChildren.org to keep current on this and other subjects.

The AAP is an organization of 64,000 primary-care pediatricians, pediatric medical subspecialists, and pediatric surgical specialists dedicated to the health and well-being of all infants, children, adolescents, and young adults. The information in these pages explains the child developmental process that can leave parents and their young children feeling good about the entire process of toilet training and what they have accomplished.

It is the AAP's hope that *Guide to Toilet Training* will continue to be an invaluable resource and reference guide for parents and caregivers, along with the guidance of your child's pediatrician. This book puts toilet training into perspective. Our intent is to enable parents and their young children to positively experience the child's ability to develop control of her/his bodily functions. We hope to provide parents with the knowledge and skills that enable their children to be successfully toilet-trained and to feel good about their accomplishment.

Karen Remley, MD, MBA, MPH, FAAP
CEO/Executive Director

American Academy of Pediatrics
# GUIDE TO TOILET TRAINING

## CHAPTER 1

# TOILET TRAINING: A NATURAL PART OF GROWING UP

"We've only just started toilet-training our son, Andrew, and already I'm confused," writes Linda, the mother of a two-year-old. "As far as I can tell, we've done everything right. Four weeks ago my husband and I bought Andrew his own potty, explained what it was, and put it in the bathroom. He didn't show any interest in using it—except as a hat—and we were careful not to pressure him.

"Then this morning when he woke up, I finally gave in to temptation and asked him if he might want to use the potty today. He looked at me and then started to cry! I couldn't understand what I'd said to upset him. I didn't know how to react, so I just gave him a hug and said, 'Okay, honey, you don't have to.' But I wish someone could tell me what's going on."

If you are the parent of a young child in diapers, you may share Linda's uncertainty over how best to begin toilet training. You are probably concerned about putting too much pressure on your child by starting too early, or letting him down by starting too late. You may be confused by conflicting advice in the media, on the web, and from relatives and friends, telling you that you can toilet-train your child by his first birthday. Or you may have been told that you should wait until your child is three or four, that you can "train in a day," or that training should take place gradually over several months to a year. Or you might have read that a parent-enforced routine of regular potty sessions is the best way to train a child, or that it's better to let the child decide when, where, and how he will go. As if this weren't enough, your child's own evolving urges and needs can suddenly derail even the simplest, most positive toilet-training program. Your family situation—marital stress, a recent move to another home, or a new baby in the family—may affect your child's progress in ways you hadn't predicted, while your own feelings or memories from childhood may color your attitude toward toilet training and, indirectly, that of your child.

## Common Questions and Concerns

Most likely, what you are looking for when approaching the toilet-training process are simple answers to two basic questions:

- "When should I start?"
- "What method should I use?"

Many people you ask are willing to provide you with cut-and-dry responses to these questions. However, their advice may not be appropriate for *your* family or, most important, for *your* child. Some children are ready to start toilet training at eighteen months, while others will learn more quickly and easily if given more time to be developmentally ready. Many children respond well to a regular potty routine, but yours may resist using the potty at the same time every day, and prefer to wait until he feels the need to go. The truth is that nearly any approach to toilet training will get the job done sooner or later, but an approach specially tailored to your child's stage of development and learning style will take you both through the process in the most positive, efficient way. By learning how to evaluate your child's readiness for toilet training, you will be able to start the process at the best possible time for her.

In this book, you will learn to find your own answers to the questions "When should I start toilet-training my child?" and "What method should I use?" You will learn which basic skills your child must acquire before true bathroom mastery can occur. You will become familiar with a variety of verbal, physical, social, and other approaches to teaching your child about potty use, and discover ways to mix and match these techniques to suit your child's personality, temperament, and evolving needs. If you find yourself defeated by your child's resistance to training, you will also find information about what may be causing the problem—along with encouragement to discard methods that aren't working and guidance on when to try a new approach.

Above all, you will be encouraged to look at toilet training not as a grueling if necessary part of parenting a young child but as an early opportunity to familiarize yourself with your child's developing personality and to find out how he learns best. When you think about it, toilet use is one of the first

and most significant skills your child must acquire consciously, rather than in response to the kinds of instinctive
urges that prompted him to learn to walk or talk.

In fact, there is nothing instinctive about using the potty.
It is a practice that your child adopts for reasons such as you
want him to use it and he wants to please you. To teach him
this habit, you must consistently encourage him, monitor his
progress, and reward him for success. You must observe his
responses to your training techniques and adapt your approach accordingly. You must support your child in his earli-
est efforts to set goals for himself and consistently meet them.
In the process you may discover that your child learns best
through verbal interaction (talking about potty use rather
than simply imitating and practicing) or that he responds to
learning by doing (sitting on the potty at scheduled times so
that potty use becomes a regular part of his routine). You may
find that he appreciates tactful reminders or stubbornly resists them, that he is happiest when allowed to demonstrate
every step of his progress or that he prefers practicing behind
closed doors.

These discoveries, which enhance your understanding of
your young child and help you to teach him how to learn,
offer benefits beyond just learning to use the toilet. They lay
the groundwork for you to connect with your child in positive ways—and set the tone for efficient learning in the years
to come.

The key to toilet training—and, yes, the *fun* of it—lies in
choosing the time and techniques that work best in your family, teaching yourself to use them effectively and consistently,
and observing your child's amazing progress as he responds
to a "lesson plan" designed for him alone.

## WHAT TOILET TRAINING SHOULD BE

- A natural result of your child's developmental readiness
- An opportunity to observe your child's progress in every aspect of his growth
- A chance to find out how your child learns best and to practice communicating effectively
- A way for your child to experience the pleasure of formulating a goal, working toward it, and achieving success
- A way to reinforce your child's confidence and self-esteem

### When to Toilet-Train: Is There a "Right" Age?

"Susan's nearly three and still in diapers? Hmmm. I had every one of my kids trained by eighteen months, and they never even wet the bed after that."

Wouldn't you like to have a nickel for every time you've heard a comment like this? If you have been subject to such remarks, chances are they came from a member of an older generation who parented at a time when early training was popular.

It is easy for adults with grown children to forget the many accidents and regressions that almost certainly followed such early training. It is also true that toilet training was defined differently back then compared to how we view it now. One-year-olds were placed on the potty after meals, for instance, and held there until they eliminated. Such procedures are based on conditioning rather than real learning—more like housebreaking a pet than helping a child achieve self-mastery!

While a one-year-old may have eventually learned to connect sitting on the potty with urinating or passing stool, success still depended on the adult's noting that it was time for potty use, physically placing the child on the potty, and keeping her there until she eliminated. Additional skills that a fully toilet-trained child must acquire—the ability to recognize her need to use the bathroom, wait until she gets to a toilet, lower her pants, and sit long enough to achieve success—depend on cognitive, emotional, and physiological developments that usually emerge only after about age eighteen to twenty-four months. For that reason, it is better to see your role as a parent as an "enabler" rather than a "trainer."

The truth is that most popular assumptions about the best age to toilet-train—in this and most other countries—depend more on the adults' needs, desires, and cultural attitudes than on a typical child's readiness to control her bodily functions. For example:

- In many African and South American cultures, where mothers and babies stay in almost constant physical contact and babies don't wear diapers, mothers "train" their babies from an early age by positioning them over whatever place they wish them to eliminate into the moment they sense that the child is about to void.

- In Finland and other northern European countries, children are traditionally placed on the potty after a feeding from infancy onward—and if the child happens to urinate or defecate while she's held there, she is praised.

The pressures of two working parents or single parents who work have increased the desire to get toilet training accomplished as soon as possible. While many daycare and preschool programs will help facilitate the toilet-training process, some make toilet training a requisite for admission.

Generally speaking, if you initiate toilet training before eighteen months, then you should also have realistic expectations for your child's performance. Child development experts now believe that toilet training works best for most families if it can be delayed until the child is ready to control much of the process herself.

Successful toilet training can help a child gain independence and self-confidence.

## VARIATION IN READINESS AMONG CHILDREN

Children younger than twelve months of age not only are unlikely to be ready in terms of bladder and bowel control but also may not yet have the physical skills needed to get to the potty and remove their clothing in time. For these young children, there is also the question of emotional readiness—that is, do they have the desire to use a potty, including a positive attitude toward the training process, and the ability to manage any bathroom-related fears?

This emotional readiness may not occur until age two, three, or four years in some children, or it may come and go as your child grows. Her verbal abilities, which enable her to learn through conversation and instruction and to express any fears or anxieties that arise, may start to expand quickly only at age two or three. Even the social awareness that motivates some children to imitate their siblings' or playmates' bathroom use increases steadily through the toddler years and into preschool.

Each of these aspects of development occurs at different times in different children, and you are

### When to Toilet-Train: The Right Reasons

If you are thinking of starting toilet training now, take a moment to consider your reasons for this decision. Do you

the best judge of when your child has acquired enough of the necessary physical, social, emotional, and cognitive skills to begin training. You or other members of your family may also find that you yourselves are better able to manage the training process at one time than at another—a period when you are not feeling particularly stressed, when you have time off work, or when you do not foresee major changes at home. Since the fluctuations in a child's development and her family's situation are impossible to predict, it's best to avoid assuming that your child will begin training by a certain age. Instead, consider taking the readiness approach—that is, reading in the following chapters about the telltale signs of readiness, looking for them in your child, and only then beginning training, regardless of your child's age. In general, the longer you wait before beginning toilet training, the easier and quicker the process is likely to be since your child will have become more self-sufficient. Still, even toddlers can learn to use the potty quite easily during periods when their natural negativity has abated somewhat and they are highly motivated to learn.

feel that your child is prepared to start—and to succeed at this challenging process? Has she expressed an interest? Do you need to move her out of diapers soon due to childcare requirements or financial pressure? Or are you simply feeling uneasy because other children her age or younger have already been toilet-trained, because your older child was already trained by this age, or because relatives or friends are beginning to ask you when you're going to start?

These last few motivators can be quite powerful, but they are best ignored. Your child's needs have little to do with those of her peers or siblings. Even twins frequently become ready for toilet training at very different times. Other children's training schedules should therefore not be a consideration, nor should the understandable but counterproductive desire to demonstrate your parenting skills or your child's advanced intelligence. Rest assured: many brilliant children, even those with wonderful, loving parents, do not become fully trained until preschool or even later.

## How to Toilet-Train: What's Best for Your Child

Just as every parent has a different opinion about when it's best to begin toilet training, every parent you know is likely to recommend a different training method that worked best for their child. You may have heard that demonstrating toilet use for your child is a good way to help him learn through imitation. A friend may have told you that all she had to do with her son was read him a book about potty use and talk it over with him. Many parents recommend talking with their children about toilet use and then asking every two hours, "Do you need to go?" Some feel that rewarding a child with gold stars on a chart or a small treat is the most effective method. Timing is also a factor, as some parents prefer a brief, concentrated approach (perhaps even taking time off from work to deliver two weeks of "immersion training"), while others feel that their children are less pressured when allowed to adjust to potty use gradually over many months.

Any of these approaches may work well with your child. But keep in mind that it is not necessary to choose a single method—in fact, your child will benefit from a combination of verbal, physical, social, and other forms of training no matter what his age. In this book you will be encouraged to choose from an array of effective toilet-training techniques according to your child's and your own personalities, interests, and needs.

Even the most sensible, standard methods may fail to apply to a particular child, as Linda learned with her son, Andrew, whose reaction was described at the opening of this chapter. In Linda's case, Andrew happened to be passing through one of the typical resistant periods of toddlerhood in which the urge to control his own behavior was irresistibly strong. Though Linda was careful not to pressure her son to use the potty, he could easily sense her eagerness to see him do so. The conflict he felt between his desire to dictate his own actions and his desire to please his mother increased

## A PARENT'S STORY

### No Two Are the Same

"I have three children. One was completely trained before age three. My son was trained at four and a half and my other daughter by three and a half. What I learned from this is that each child is unique. It's important not to make the child feel like he's bad if he doesn't 'get' toilet training right when you want him to, and not to compare one child to another."

Rose, mother of Jacob, Tessa, and Molly

each time he noticed the potty in the bathroom—until Linda's casual suggestion that he try using the potty caused him to burst into tears.

Linda responded wisely by altering her training plan—in this case, backing off and just ignoring the potty for a while. As a result, Andrew gradually began to experiment at his own pace and soon, with Linda's praise and support, began using the potty regularly.

Accepting and adjusting to your child's personal style can make toilet training a much less stressful experience than you

## ASK YOURSELF

### How Do You Feel About Toilet Training?

Children learn any new skill most easily when they sense their parents' confident, positive attitude toward the process. You may find it helpful, then, to consider your feelings about excretion, diaper changing, accidents, and other issues related to bathroom use as you start thinking about how best to toilet-train your child. If you find it embarrassing to discuss elimination or to demonstrate using the toilet to your child, he is likely to pick up on your discomfort. Such impressions may lead him to believe that potty use is an unpleasant activity or that his private parts are "bad" or shameful. You may want to talk these feelings through with your partner, friends who have young children, your pediatrician, or even a professional therapist before beginning training.

may have expected. You may also find yourself getting to know your child in a way you didn't before, appreciating his special qualities, becoming familiar with his emerging interests, and respecting him as a unique, interesting individual.

## Training with Confidence: Creating Your Plan

In the following chapters you will learn what to look for to determine whether your child is ready for toilet training. You will read about the basic steps that must be taken to

The same holds true for any negative feelings you have about diaper changing, cleaning up after accidents, or watching your child fail to accomplish a new skill many times before he gets it right. If you know that you have difficulty managing your emotions when messes and repeated failures occur, think ahead about how you will handle these situations. A decision to count to ten before you become overwhelmed about a mistake, to make a joke out of the situation, or to simply step out of the room for a moment will not only save your child from feelings of inadequacy but also teach him that it's possible to manage frustration or disappointment in positive ways. Meanwhile, make an effort not to judge your child for his mistakes—after all, everyone makes mistakes when learning a new skill. This will prepare you to support him more effectively in the years to come.

teach any child to use the potty on her own. You will find descriptions of particular techniques that work well for many children, as well as suggestions on how to resolve the problems that toilet-training children and their families commonly face.

You will also find special tips for parents training older children and those training children with special needs. Causes of post-toilet-training problems with elimination will be discussed. Finally, you will find information on managing bedwetting, which can continue beyond preschool into the elementary school years.

These are the tools you will need to create your own toilet-training plan and implement it at the best time for your child. But there are certain universal rules relating to toilet training—as well as to other aspects of parenting—that will enhance your and your family's experience no matter what method you choose. These are important and include:

- **Be positive.** Children learn best when they are praised for their progress rather than punished for their mistakes. Do what you can to help your child succeed as often as possible—even if it means learning gradually, one tiny step at a time. When she progresses, give her a hug, some praise, and perhaps even a small tangible reward. When she fails, tell her you're sure she'll do better next time and ask her to help you clean up.

- **Try to be as consistent as possible.** Create reasonable expectations according to your child's abilities, express them clearly and frequently, and expect your child to at least try to follow them every time. Keep her bathroom routine as consistent as possible, with her potty in the same place every day and the sequence of actions, including wiping and hand washing, the same every time. While she is toilet training, praise your child for each success, and provide predictable, nonpunitive consequences (such as helping to clean up) for each failure. Make sure that your approach to toilet training is consistent with those of your child's other caregivers as well.

- **Stay involved and observe.** Very young children's needs, behaviors, and abilities change frequently and, to some extent, unpredictably. Toilet-training approaches that worked two weeks ago may not work today, and skills that your child mastered in the past may temporarily disappear in the face of new challenges. Continue to monitor your child's bathroom behavior throughout toilet training and afterward so that you can quickly identify and resolve any new problems that arise.

- **Enjoy.** Toilet training is a necessary chore, but it can also be fun at times. Don't take your child's hesitations, passing fears, or resistance too seriously. Nearly every child learns to use the toilet sooner or later, and your child will, too. Do what you can to occasionally take your eye off the long-term goal and enjoy the charming, funny moments along the way.

If you are concerned that designing a training plan to suit your particular child may prove more difficult than following a prepackaged, one-size-fits-all program, keep in mind that it doesn't take a great deal of effort to discern whether your child is more a talker or a doer, more a lover of adult-imposed routine or an independent soul who prefers to control her own actions. In the process of figuring that out, you and your child will have gotten to know each other better. Furthermore, your child will have learned a new skill in a way that increased her confidence, her sense of security, and her self-esteem. What a wonderful process to have been a part of!

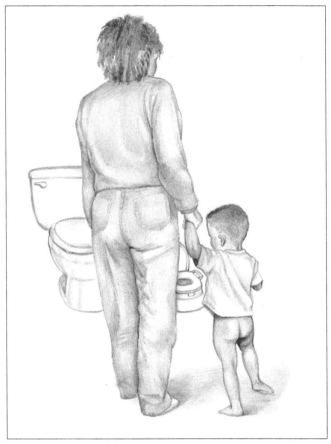

While there are many different strategies parents can use when toilet-training their children, all should include as much parental involvement and encouragement as possible.

# Q & A

## Toilet Training: What Can We Expect?

**Q:** How long does it usually take to toilet-train a child?

**A:** The answer depends in part on how you define the beginning of the process (when you first introduce the potty? When your child first sits on it? When he first uses it successfully?) and the end (when your child has associated the potty with his need to eliminate? When he has stopped wearing diapers? When he no longer wets the bed at night?). In cases when a child is physiologically and cognitively ready for toilet training (see Chapter 2), the basic training process, from sitting on the potty to using it with some regularity, usually takes around six weeks. However, your child is likely to experience many accidents and even regressions after this period, and may not be fully dry at night for several more years.

**Q:** My one-year-old is interested in the potty and seems ready to start toilet training. Are there negative psychological consequences related to starting this early?

**A:** As long as you limit your expectations and withhold negative judgment, there is certainly no harm in responding to your child's interest in the potty and how it's used. Your one-year-old may be cognitively ready to make the necessary connections, and physiological readiness will follow soon enough. Meanwhile, responding to his curiosity and casually presenting him with the next step in the process will show him that you take his interests seriously and appreciate his desire to learn. Be aware, however, that your child's interest in the toilet may start to fade as the development of other skills takes up more of his energy and attention. This is natural, and he will come back to toilet training again when he is ready.

**Q:**    People often act surprised and even disapproving when they learn that my four-year-old is still in diapers. I haven't trained him yet because he hasn't shown an interest, and I don't want to force the issue on him against his will. Is there any real deadline for toilet training?

**A:**    The average age for toilet training in this country is currently between two and three years. This is why children trained earlier are frequently considered "advanced" (though there is no relation between age of toilet training and a child's intelligence), while those not trained by age four may be looked down upon. While no child should be pressured to do something just for the purpose of keeping up with his peers, your child may become aware of the disapproval of others, which can have a negative effect on his self-esteem. If you see signs that your child is beginning to feel bad about himself, you may want to initiate the training even before he expresses any interest. Chances are he's ready. He may just be waiting for more active encouragement from you.

Toilet training can and should be a positive and rewarding experience for both parent and child.

## CHAPTER 2

# HOW TO TELL WHEN
# YOUR CHILD IS READY

Lindy, two and a half, has recently begun demonstrating many of the signs of readiness for toilet training. When she senses that she's about to wet her diaper, she gets a funny look on her face and sometimes drops into a squatting position. When she's about to have a bowel movement, she runs and hides behind the couch. She has even figured out how to get her diaper off and loves to run around the house naked whenever she gets the chance.

Lindy's parents agree that this seems to be the perfect time to start. Yet when they point out the potty in the bathroom to Lindy and suggest that she sit on it for a while, she just laughs and runs away. She'd rather risk an accident—and her parents' annoyance—than sit still long enough to use the bathroom.

Determining the best time to begin toilet training is not always easy. Readiness occurs at different ages for different children, and your own child may be ready in one area of development but not in another. A one-year-old who happily sits on her potty to look at picture books still may not be able to comprehend the potty's real purpose, while a two-year-old who knows what potties are for may refuse to use his out of a toddler's natural desire to remain in almost constant motion.

In general, most children become physiologically ready for toilet training at around eighteen months of age—that is, their digestive system and bladder have matured to the point where they can delay a bowel movement or urination long enough to get to a potty. But they are usually not cognitively ready—able to associate the need to eliminate with potty use, to remember to use it, and to resist distraction long enough to complete the process—until sometime after their second birthday.

The motor skills needed to get to the bathroom, manage clothes, and sit still on the potty are also clearly important. So is the emotional urge toward independence and self-mastery—as well as sufficient emotional maturity to relax control sufficiently to avoid constipation. Social readiness—an awareness of others' toilet use and a desire to imitate their behavior—is a powerful motivating force for toddlers and preschoolers. Another factor is the verbal ability to understand your explanations of how toilet use works and to communicate to you any confusion or uneasiness they feel.

As you can see, a range of physical and psychological developments help support the process of toilet training. While it isn't necessary to wait until you're sure that every one of these developments is in place, each step does increase the chances of toilet-training success. In this chapter you'll learn to recognize the behaviors that signal your child's readiness and suggest ways to take advantage of them as they appear.

## EARLY SIGNS OF READINESS

Look for any of the following signs that your child is ready:

- Your child stays dry at least two hours at a time during the day or is dry after naps.
- Your child's bowel movements become regular and predictable, and any constipation issues are addressed and under control.
- Facial expressions, posture, or words reveal that your child is about to urinate or have a bowel movement.
- Your child can follow simple instructions.
- Your child can walk to and from the bathroom and help undress himself.
- Your child seems uncomfortable with soiled diapers and wants to be changed.
- Your child asks to use the toilet or potty.
- Your child asks to wear "big-kid" underwear.

## "Gotta Go!": Physiological Readiness and Motor Skills

All parents are familiar with the routine of feeding breast milk or formula to a baby and then immediately changing her diaper after her meal. At times the diaper-wetting response occurs so quickly that it seems the milk or formula has gone into one end of the baby and straight through to the diaper at the other end. This involuntary elimination process occurs because a baby's digestive system has not yet fully matured.

While urine fills the baby's bladder and is released th]
urethra, and bowel movements fill the large intestin
expelled via the rectum, just as with adults, babies cannot yet
control the circular sphincter muscles that keep the bladder
and rectum closed. As a baby's stomach fills during a feeding
and passes more fluid to the bladder, the sphincter muscles
automatically relax, and urination or a bowel movement occurs. As long as this process remains involuntary, until at least
eighteen months of age in most cases, a baby is unable to
consciously delay elimination. If placed on a potty at the right
time, she will void into it, but she cannot deliberately wait to
use the potty and so cannot be fully toilet-trained.

## PARENT POTTY TIPS

Patience is the best approach. When your
child is ready, they will make the decision
and let you know. Ultimately rewards only
take you so far. And punishment is not going
to work. When the child is ready for the
potty, they will show interest, and that's
when you should start. Trying before they
are ready just causes stress and frustration,
and will delay progress.

### Awareness of the Need to Go

At around her first birthday, your child will begin to recognize the sensation of a full rectum or bladder, signaling a
need to eliminate. In many cases your child will show her
awareness through her behavior: squatting and grunting
when she is about to have a bowel movement or tugging at
her diaper when she needs to urinate. Even though she will
still not be able to delay the function that she senses is taking

place, it is a good idea to reinforce this awareness of the link between the inner feeling of fullness and the act of excretion or urination.

When you see that she is about to eliminate, your comment should be a neutral one: "Oops, I think a poop [or pee] is coming. Do you feel it happening?" Once she has soiled or wet her diaper, change it right away to reinforce the concept that bowel movements and urine should be removed from the body and discarded. Remember, this is a natural process, and there is no need to comment negatively about it (words such as *dirty* or *messy* will only make your child feel bad), but you can certainly say positive things about how good it feels and smells to be clean and dry. Your goal is to strengthen your child's awareness of the feeling of needing to go so that she can build on this understanding when the time comes. Encourage her to see toilet training as a desirable skill.

## Bowel and Bladder Control

Usually at around eighteen months of age or a little later, your child will begin to gain some control of her sphincter muscles. When that happens, she can delay excretion for brief periods of time. This increased control is a gradual process that takes place over months and sometimes years, usually beginning with nighttime bowel control, moving to daytime bowel and bladder control, and finally achieving nighttime bladder control. Even older children may occasionally experience bedwetting and other accidents because the development of this voluntary muscle control is still incomplete. But her ability to delay a daytime bowel movement— however briefly—will allow you to begin introducing your child to the concept of potty use, as long as she shows an interest and does not resist your efforts.

First, look for signs that this development is occurring in your child. Such signs may include running to hide behind the couch or shutting herself in her room when she feels the need to eliminate, or she might wait until her diaper is on (or off) to have a bowel movement or urinate.

A child will start to recognize the feeling of a full bladder around his first birthday and will signal his awareness through behavior such as squatting, grunting, pulling at his pants or diaper, jumping up and down, or whimpering.

If your child has begun to demonstrate these or similar behaviors, now might be a good time to purchase a potty, briefly describe its use to your child, and place it in the bathroom for possible use. Since physiological readiness is only a first, early step toward toilet training, chances are good that she will not yet want to use the potty for elimination (though she might be happy using it as a chair). Still, now that the potty is present, you might have the opportunity to place her on it as soon as you see her squatting, grunting, or clutching her pants. If she happens to wait to eliminate until after she's sitting on the potty, you will have helped her begin to associate bowel movements with potty use.

While these first steps toward potty awareness are not usually sufficient for complete toilet training, each positive experience in this area does lay the groundwork for quicker comprehension once more development has occurred.

## A PARENT'S STORY

### Starting to Squat a Lot

"Our son's babysitter was the first to notice his physical readiness for toilet training—even before we'd gotten around to buying him a potty. She saw how he'd stop whatever he was doing and squat down about half a minute before he made a bowel movement, so she started just whisking him into the bathroom in time for him to go. He didn't seem to mind, and I think it really helped him associate his physical feeling with the bathroom. We didn't start to toilet-train him for another six months, but once we did we couldn't believe how quickly it happened. He seemed to have figured out a lot of it on his own."

Sandy, mother of Allen

## Motor Skills

In addition to your child's physiological development, his motor skills must reach a certain level of maturity before he can easily begin toilet training. The ability to walk (beginning at around twelve months) is an obvious asset in getting to the potty in time to use it. During the early months of learning to walk, your child's preoccupation with practicing this new skill will probably leave little energy for experimenting with potty use. As he grows more comfortable with getting around on two legs, however (by around eighteen to twenty-four months), he may become interested in acquiring other "grown-up" skills. Throughout the process it is helpful to praise what he does well (such as "I like the way you can sit on the potty").

Teaching a child of eighteen to thirty-six months to dress and undress herself, or making sure her clothing is easy to remove, can help facilitate toilet training.

The gradual improvement in other gross and fine motor skills, which usually begins at around eighteen months, will support your child's ability to handle his clothing more efficiently and to engage in activities that may keep him seated on the potty long enough to eliminate successfully. You can encourage these developments by teaching him to dress and undress himself, making sure that his clothing is easy to remove, and offering him picture books, toys, or crayons and paper to play with while he's waiting for a bowel movement to occur. The ability to master all of these new skills also greatly enhances a young child's self-esteem—confidence that comes in handy as he meets the toilet-training challenge.

### "What Does This Do?": Cognitive and Verbal Readiness

If you know how to ride a bicycle, you probably remember how hard it was to master this skill. First you had to learn how to steer and to pedal. Next you had to put these two skills together while trying to keep your balance, and learn how to do it smoothly.

During the toilet-training process, your child must learn to coordinate a complex combination of physical and cognitive tasks, much the way we do when we attempt to learn a new skill such as riding a bicycle. She must familiarize herself with the necessary "equipment" (her body and its functions), associate physical sensations with the proper responses, picture what she wants to do (use the potty), create a plan to get there, begin using it, and remain in place long enough to finish, which requires both memory and concentration. Throughout this learning process, she must be able to understand your explanations, commands, and responses to some extent.

---

PARENT POTTY TIPS

If toilet training is making life impossible, adjust the strategies to make them work for your family. Consistency is the most important part of toilet training, and when life doesn't allow for consistency, you have to forgive yourself and find another way to support your child.

---

## Body Awareness

Clearly, all of this learning takes time. The first steps in this process involve bodily sensation—the ability to associate an inner feeling of fullness with the bowel movement or urination that results—and usually take place at around twelve to eighteen months. Your efforts to reinforce this awareness by remarking on the poop or pee to come are among the first productive actions you can take to start your child thinking about potty use.

As time passes, your child may demonstrate discomfort over a dirty diaper; she may also try to remove her diaper or resist being diapered, and otherwise show that her awareness of her physical state is expanding. She may start to enjoy (and even insist on) spending a substantial amount of time without clothes on, and by age two will have become quite interested in all of her body parts, especially the "private" ones used to eliminate. This is the age when boys commonly begin to talk about their penis, or comment on Dad's, while girls start to explore and ask questions about the vagina and its uses. Such interest in the body indicates a new openness to your explanations of how the body works and a desire to "name the equipment."

Acquiring simple words to describe your child's body and its workings helps your child think more fully about the process of elimination. It also sets the stage for learning through experience. Just letting her sit on the potty until she happens to have a bowel movement—and then hearing you say how pleased you are by what she did—is likely to help your child connect the need to poop with potty use more effectively than any long-winded explanation.

## Making Plans and Carrying Them Out

Understanding the link between needing to eliminate and doing so is an important first step in toilet-training readiness. Still, more development is necessary before your child can begin picturing the potty when she needs to go, plan how she will get to the bathroom and urinate into the potty, and re-member her plan long enough to carry it out. These next steps in the developmental process require the capacity for pictur-ing actions (symbolic thought), planning (problem solving), and memory—abilities that begin to surface at age one but become much better established by age two or even later.

One of the first signs that your child is able to think of an object when it isn't there, for example, is at around twelve months, when she begins to wail every time you leave the room. For the first time, she can picture you and know that you con-tinue to exist even though she can't get to you, and it is the frustration caused by this understanding that makes her cry.

In the coming months, her brain will develop to the point where she realizes she can crawl or toddle to the next room to find you—and walk to the bathroom to find her potty. By age two she may routinely picture her potty when she needs to use the bathroom. She may even know how to find the potty when she wants to. She may still need your support, however, in making the associations required to decide to go to the potty when she feels the urge and accomplishing her mission before other thoughts or events distract her.

## THROUGH A CHILD'S EYES

### "What Happened?"

Maria is sitting on her potty, paging through an oversized picture book that rests on her lap. She has removed every stitch of clothing, and her mother, resigned to this temporary behavior, has decided to look the other way for now. As Maria traces a picture in the book with one hand, her other hand reaches underneath to explore the parts of her body that are usually covered by a diaper. Suddenly she has that funny feeling . . . pee, she thinks. Then her hand is wet.

"Mommy!" Maria yells. The book slides off her lap, and Maria stands up. Her mother arrives and, when she sees what's happened, says, "Maria, you peed in your potty! Good job! Let's wash your hands and then we'll read your favorite book together."

Maria frowns. There's pee in the potty. She doesn't understand what happened exactly. But she realizes that making pee and sitting on the potty are somehow connected, and that this event makes Mommy happy. She files the experience away as Mom washes her hands, and then she moves on to find her favorite book.

## TOILET-TRAINING THOUGHTS

Here are some guidelines and suggestions to help guide you through the toilet-training process. Each of them is discussed in more detail elsewhere in this chapter.

- Readiness for toilet training occurs at different ages in different children. But most children are physiologically ready for toilet training at about eighteen months of age.
- Adopt and use simple words to describe your child's body and its workings for use when discussing issues related to toilet training with your child.
- Offer your child picture books, toys, or crayons and paper to occupy him while he's sitting on the toilet and waiting for a bowel movement to occur.
- Verbally praise your child when he does something good related to his toilet training.
- Keep in mind that your child's desire to control his physical functions may increase during times of major changes in his life.

By age two and a half or three, your child's evolving interest in problem solving will support her ability to accomplish this series of actions on her own. Solving problems requires picturing a solution and planning a way to achieve it, and seeing these skills develop is perhaps one of the most pleasurable ways of noting that your child is approaching toilet-training readiness. As your child moves from her second birthday to her third, you will be able to observe her solving problems over and over, all day long—from how to get her toy shovel back from another child in the sandbox to how to get you to give her an extra piece of her favorite treat after dinner. The sight of your child's pensive face, pondering how she will obtain the current object of her desire, is a sure sign that she is also cognitively mature enough to figure out how to solve the problem of staying dry without diapers ("I need to go to the bathroom and sit on the potty now").

## More Complex Thinking

A number of other cognitive developments greatly facilitate your child's ability to use the potty successfully beginning at around age two and a half or three. Her memory will have improved a great deal, enabling her not only to remember where she is headed when she starts toward the bathroom but also to recall previous toilet-training experiences and benefit from them. Her imagination has expanded, allowing her to explore potty use through imaginary play with stuffed animals, dolls, and puppets. (An expanded imagination may also create new problems in toilet training, leading to anxieties such as the fear of a flushing toilet or the fear of being flushed away.) By age three she will have grown somewhat better at interrupting her focus on another task to go to the bathroom and resist distraction on the way. Chances are she will have achieved the verbal sophistication necessary to communicate any problems or confusion that she is experiencing.

These essential cognitive and verbal developments, just as important to toilet training success as physiological growth, are the reason most parents find that waiting until age two to three years to begin training usually makes the process much easier. Particularly if you have begun laying the groundwork at an earlier age, waiting for your child's natural development to fall into place can be a wise decision.

---

## A PARENT'S STORY

### Talk About It!

"For months before we started actively toilet-training our youngest son, we talked matter-of-factly about using the toilet, in all kinds of ways. Only at about twenty-four months did he start to give an understanding nod. Still, we believe our talking facilitated the process enormously by giving him a chance to think about elimination and imagine using the potty before he tried to do it."

Bruce, father of Johnny

---

### "I Can Do It!": Emotional Growth and Social Awareness

For many parents, a child's emotional readiness for toilet training is the most difficult to recognize—particularly since a child moves in and out of emotional "prime times" and troublesome periods for toilet training throughout early childhood. Emotional issues that can profoundly affect toilet training include the following:

- A desire for independence and self-mastery
- The child's need to control some aspects of his environment
- Testing of limits and rules
- His desire to win his parents' approval
- Fears associated with toilet use
- Desire to mimic or conform to other children's behavior

The best way to determine the emotional state your child is in, and how conducive this is to toilet training, is to observe both his general behavior and his responses to your suggestions about potty use. If he clearly enjoys sitting on his potty or talking about potty use, his urge toward self-mastery will probably support his training. If he resists the idea or cries when you mention the potty, he may be experiencing conflict and you will need to wait for a more opportune time.

### Self-Mastery

The desire to master one's own body and environment is a powerful desire common to all toddlers and preschoolers. The onset of cries of "I did it!" will let you know that your two-year-old's urge toward independence is in full swing. On one hand, this type of ambition can inspire great toilet-training progress as your child tries to act like a big kid in every possible way. Periodically, however, his need to control his own body and environment may manifest itself in less-than-desirable ways.

Your two-year-old may insist on running away and hiding each time he feels the urge to have a bowel movement, in an effort to prevent you from picking him up and placing him on the potty. He may even get up off the potty and have an accident on the living room floor. At age two he may yell

"No!" whenever you ask him if he needs to go, or delay going until it's too late and an accident occurs. The more attention you give such experiments—all normal attempts to test your rules and limits—the more he will repeat them. The best response is to clean up the mess, keep your comments minimal, downplay the incident, and wait for a later, more mature phase of independence to inspire him to show you what a "big boy" he can be.

To help this process along, consider allowing your child to watch siblings or parents use a toilet or potty. This can take place in your home, or perhaps they can observe other children use the potty in a daycare setting.

Observing a sibling using the toilet can result in a child's show of readiness to toilet-train.

## Resistance

Your child's desires to control his physical functions and his environment may increase during times of major change in his life. A child who feels disoriented by recent upsets (such as a move to a new house, a divorce, or the arrival of a new baby in the home) may seek to regain balance by exerting tighter control over those aspects of life that are within reach. Inner stresses, such as fears resulting from a rapidly developing imagination, may also lead to resistant behavior that makes toilet training difficult. Older toddlers and preschoolers, who are physiologically able to delay bladder or bowel movements longer when desired, can deliberately withhold stool and become seriously constipated in response to stress, parental pressure, or even reluctance to let go of what they experience as a part of their bodies.

Again, when you are confronted with such resistance, it's best to back off for a while. With your help, your child will soon pass out of this emotional stage, and you can readdress toilet-training issues when he's better prepared to do so.

## Desire for Approval

Two of the greatest tools that parents can take advantage of during toilet training are their child's desire for approval and his urge to imitate others' behavior. Your child's experiments with winning your approval probably began before his first birthday. Spurred on by cognitive development to explore cause-and-effect relationships ("I bite Mommy's nose and what happens?"), he soon begins to assemble a database of which types of actions win positive responses from you and which do not. The more smiles and words of parental praise your child experiences during childhood development, the more likely they will serve as a reinforcement for him to continue with them and make great efforts to please you.

Throughout the toddler and preschool years, praising your child for any small step toward bathroom mastery will pave the way for faster, more positive training. If your child has not been successfully toilet-trained by age three and a half, his renewed desire to please can make adapting to potty use quite simple, for this is an age when many of his issues around independence will have been resolved.

## IT'S BEST NOT TO TOILET-TRAIN WHEN . . .

- Your child is constipated
- A new baby is due soon or has recently joined your household
- Your family has recently moved to a new home
- Your child is in a new childcare situation or has recently started preschool
- You and your partner have recently separated or are having serious marital problems
- Your child is experiencing frequent bad dreams or other anxiety
- Your child's sleep schedule is irregular
- Your child is in a resistant or "negative" phase

In later chapters we will discuss ways to tap into this desire to please through affirmation ("Look what a great job you did!"), sticker charts, and other forms of positive reinforcement.

PARENT POTTY TIPS

Trust yourself! This is about the process, not the pressure. Try to enjoy the small moments of wonder and laughter as you go. These will be fun stories to tell at high school graduation!

## Social Awareness

Social awareness—the observation of and desire to be like others—gradually expands throughout the toddler and preschool years, adding yet another motivator for your child to become fully toilet-trained. At around eighteen months your child is likely to become fascinated by the behavior of other children his age or a little older, and his desire to imitate them may spur him to use the toilet much earlier than he otherwise would. (This is why children with older siblings are often toilet-trained earlier than an only child.) By age two and a half or three, he will become interested in the concept of gender and focus on imitating the behavior of his same-sex parent.

As we will soon see in Chapter 3, this is a good time for parents to start inviting their same-sex child to observe them using the bathroom. If there is no adult of the same sex in your household, try asking an adult relative or friend to act as a role model. Not only will your child's curiosity be satisfied in this way, but he may decide to start trying to use the potty to "be more like" the grown-up he admires.

By the preschool years, your child's fascination with social identity and his peers' behavior will provide quite strong motivation to wear big-kid underwear and use the toilet like other children his age. If he has not already been toilet-trained by this time, peer pressure alone can motivate him to train himself. In many cases, all it takes to toilet-train a child at this age is to point out casually (never critically) that most of the other kids in his class seem to be out of diapers. Once he is aware of this, your child may choose to toilet-train himself.

---

## A PARENT'S STORY

### Big Boy Underwear

"When my son was potty-training at the age of three we gave him a stack of 'big-boy underwear' that he could choose from to wear each day. One morning I told him to go get his 'big-boy underwear,' and he came back wearing a pair of my husband's, which he had to hold up because they were so large on him. I said, 'Those are Daddy's,' and he said, 'No, these are big underwear, and I am a big boy now!'"

Kirstin, mother of Landon

---

### "I Think She's Ready. Now What?"

When describing the developmental milestones necessary for a child to begin substituting potty use for a diaper, we have estimated rough ages at which each stage of growth occurs. Yet it is important to keep in mind that these developments take place at different times for each child, and each child may be preoccupied with a different area of development at any particular moment in her growth.

## TYPICAL TIMETABLE OF CHILDHOOD DEVELOPMENT THAT SUPPORTS TOILET TRAINING

| Age | Physiological and Motor Skills | Cognitive and Verbal Development | Emotional and Social Awareness |
|---|---|---|---|
| 0–12 months | | Begins to associate cause and effect | Begins to enjoy praise and approval |
| 12–18 months | Becomes aware of the need to go | Begins to associate fullness with elimination that follows | Emerging desire to mimic other children's behavior |
| | May begin walking | May begin communicating verbally | Takes pleasure in "doing it himself" |
| 18–24 months | Early ability to briefly control sphincter muscles | Improved ability to picture a goal (using the potty) and remember it long enough to complete the act | Increased urge toward self-mastery |
| | Better able to sit still | Increased ability to understand verbal explanations | Increased desire to please parents and win praise |
| 24–36 months | Able to manage simple clothing | Improved memory helps child maintain potty routine | Takes great pleasure in increasing competence |
| | | Improved imagination allows for learning through play (dolls, role playing) | Gender awareness encourages imitation of same-sex parent's bathroom behavior |
| 3 years + | Gradual maturing of digestive system eventually leads to decrease in accidents and bedwetting by around age 5 or 6 | Improved ability to break focus to go to the toilet and to resist distraction while getting there | Peer pressure encourages toilet use; enjoys completing sticker charts and working to earn rewards |

It is best to observe your child in light of the information provided here—focusing not on your child's chronological age but on her behavior, interests, and responses to your suggestions—when deciding whether it is time to introduce a potty into your child's day-to-day routine. Keep in mind that using negative phases may interrupt or delay the toilet-training process even when your child seems ready. If you're encountering obstacles, don't worry—you can easily start over at a later date.

Fortunately, toilet training is not a process that can be successfully initiated at only one point in your child's life. As new abilities develop, understanding deepens, and emotional readiness comes and goes, understanding and adopting the habit of toilet use becomes increasingly easy. Meanwhile, your best chance at toilet training rests on keeping an eye out for the signs that an opportunity has arrived and responding appropriately.

## Q & A

### Is It Time?

**Q:**    Is it true that boys are usually toilet-trained later than girls?

**A:**    While gender itself has little to do with how early or late a child becomes fully toilet-trained, the tendency of toddler and preschool boys to be active physically may delay their training somewhat. Two large population studies show that males are delayed by approximately six months compared to girls in toilet training (population studies, however, are not always representative of individuals). Still, other factors—such as a desire for self-mastery or a desire to please the parent—may overcome such physical issues. The difference in timing between genders is less important than individual factors that are more influential on a child's readiness for toilet training.

**Q:** My two-year-old is still in diapers. She shows some interest in the toilet (that is, she wants to talk about it—what it's for and what it does), but she has no real interest in using it. She'll sit on the toilet if we ask her to, and we've explained that she should tell us when she wants to sit on it or has to go, but she really doesn't ever do that.

**A:** It sounds as though she is processing the information about potty training. Be patient and continue to allow her time to process the ideas before she acts on them. She will start connecting them to her own circumstances, and at some point in the near future she is likely to train quickly.

**Q:** Which do children accomplish first: urinating into the potty or having a bowel movement into it?

**A:** It depends on your child. Since it is easier for most children at first to urinate into a potty than to have a bowel movement into it, some children experience their first toilet-training successes when urinating. But since it is harder to delay urination, a child may take longer to urinate into the potty consistently. For this reason, most children become fully bowel-trained first even though they have been urinating into a potty—inconsistently—for a longer period of time. In general, it's best to encourage your child to go to the potty when he feels the need for either form of elimination, but not to expect him to achieve success at the same time in each area.

**Q:**    My two-year-old seems to want to use the potty, but he usually jumps up and runs off before he finishes, leaving a mess on the bathroom floor. Is there anything we can do about this, or should we just put off toilet training until he's older?

**A:**    Nearly all two-year-olds are physically active, and yours may have an especially active personality. There is no harm in delaying toilet training until he finds it easier to sit still for three to five minutes at a time. However, since you have already started training and he seems interested in continuing, you might try focusing on keeping him in place on his potty instead. When he goes to use it next time, try staying with him and chatting, reading a story, playing a simple game, or entertaining him in any other way that will help him stay in place. As we noted earlier, praising him for his appropriate behavior can help to reinforce it. Each time he remains long enough to succeed at potty use, the practice will be reinforced and he will find it easier to remain in place long enough to succeed in the future. There is no need to pressure him too much, though. Five minutes is long enough for him to sit in one place. If he jumps up to run off and leaves an accident on the floor, it is best not to focus much attention on the situation. It's better to let your child leave the potty when he wants, leaving a mess behind, rather than forcing him to sit longer than he wants. He'll be more likely to use the potty in the future if he's not forced during any part of the process.

CHAPTER 3

# ENCOURAGING YOUR
# CHILD'S PROGRESS

"Mommy, I did it!" Joey appears in the bathroom doorway, beaming proudly at his mother. Suzanne looks up from her vacuuming, hardly daring to hope.

"You used the potty, Joey?" she says, turning off the vacuum cleaner and hurrying toward the bathroom. "Let Mommy see!"

Suzanne moves past her son to take a look at the bathroom. The scene she confronts is not quite what she'd expected. Toilet paper is draped around the sink, toilet, and potty. The books Joey was looking at while sitting on the potty are strewn across the floor. Joey has urinated, Suzanne notes—but on the floor next to the potty rather than in the bowl.

Suzanne takes a deep breath. This is the third such accident in two days, and if there's one thing she doesn't like to do, it's clean up after one of these messes. She knows, however, that a positive response is the only productive one, and adjusts her expression before turning to her son.

"Pretty good job, Joey," she says in an encouraging voice.

"You tried to pee in the potty, and you almost did it. You just stood up a little too early." She gives him a quick hug. "Now, help me clean up, okay? Let Mommy show you. . . ."

Whether your child is eighteen months or three years old, eliminating into a potty rather than a more convenient diaper is likely to seem quite strange at first—a big-people's ritual with no obvious benefits aside from a parent's praise and perhaps a small treat. It is amazing to consider, then, how hard young children try to comply with their parents' need to potty-train them, simply out of a desire to please. At times their efforts may disappoint, irritate, or even puzzle you. But try to keep your child's stage of development in mind as you respond. His attempts to cope with this new self-care concept, his natural anxiety over redirecting a natural body function, and his efforts to follow quite a complex sequence of actions are bound to lead to errors now and then. Do your best to applaud his efforts and maintain a sense of humor as he masters this difficult new skill.

### What's a Potty For? The Power of Association

In Chapter 2 we discussed the importance of creating associations in your child's mind between the physical sensations that precede elimination and the act of urinating or having a bowel movement. As you begin to observe your child picking up on this association—announcing that she needs to poop, removing her diaper when it's wet, or hiding when she's about to have a bowel movement—you can step up these reminders. When you are at home with no outsiders present, make a habit of having the same-sex parent or other adult announce the need to use the bathroom and invite the child to accompany him or her to the bathroom. Encourage other members of the family to demonstrate bathroom use as well—particularly older siblings, whom toddlers and pre-schoolers love to imitate. If you have twins, invite both to observe you or another relative's bathroom use, but don't be surprised if one shows interest and the other doesn't. Eventually the other twin's interest will kick in, and by that time she may have her sibling's potty-training example to help speed her toward potty success herself. In addition, children's books about potty training may be entertaining as well as educational when learning all the ins and outs of using the potty.

Don't worry if one twin shows more interest toward the potty than the other. Eventually, after observing their sibling, the other twin's interest will kick in and both siblings will enjoy potty success.

As your child observes the elimination process, explain to her what is happening ("See, Cindy—the pee comes out of Allie and goes into the potty. Then she flushes the pee away, and she stays nice and dry. Soon you'll be able to stay dry, too").

It doesn't matter if your child doesn't understand everything you are telling her at first. Eventually the meaning of your words will start to sink in. In the meantime, be sure to avoid comparing your untrained child negatively to the toilet-trained person she is observing. Remind her instead that soon she, too, will start using the bathroom "just like a big girl"—thus inspiring her to keep trying.

During this preparatory phase of toilet training, it's important to explain and demonstrate every step of the process. Skipping steps now can create habits that may be hard to change later. Point out each time how she will need to:

- Pull down her clothing (if boys are standing, they must learn to use the fly front)
- Remain on the potty (or in front of it if he's standing to urinate) until completely finished
- Wipe carefully with toilet paper (always front to back for girls to prevent urinary tract or vaginal infections)
- Flush the toilet (if that's what she will use and she is not afraid of the noise)
- Wash and dry her hands

Explain in simple terms that we always wash our hands after we poop or pee to be sure they are clean. If your child's increasing curiosity about toilet use prompts her to try to play with her feces, you will need to calmly stop her and explain, "This is something to flush away, not to be played with." Keep in mind that your facial expression and body language are as important as what you say. Avoid implying a sense of shame or blame. Your child is highly attuned to your emotional responses and will learn that toilet use is healthy and positive or dirty and nasty, depending on what you communicate.

## WHAT WORDS TO USE

As experienced parents will tell you, it's important to decide early what words you will use with your child to describe body parts, urine, and bowel movements, since your child is likely to use these words frequently for years to come—often within hearing of teachers, caregivers, relatives, and other adults. In most cases, common, simple words are best—such as *pee* and *poop* or *number one* and *number two*. Such terms will not offend, confuse, or embarrass your child or others, and you can always teach your child the proper terms when she's older.

Be sure to avoid words such as *naughty* or *stinky,* which can make your child feel self-conscious or uneasy about the elimination process. Talking in a simple, matter-of-fact manner about bowel movements and urination will encourage your child to think matter-of-factly about bathroom use as well.

Letting a child surround his potty with his favorite toys can encourage pride of ownership and increased interest in his "special chair."

## Choosing and Installing a Potty

Once your child demonstrates an interest in or readiness for toilet training, it's time to install a potty in your home. Take your child with you to purchase this "special chair," explain to him what it will be used for, and let him help decide which one to buy. If you already have a potty chair in storage from an older sibling, you can create excitement (to help the child consider it new) by wrapping it as a present for the current child.

Encourage him to play with it, set it where he wants it, and surround it with his favorite stuffed animals, books, and toys. Pride of ownership frequently facilitates a toddler's or preschooler's interest in potty use, and its child-friendly size enables him to satisfy the powerful desire to "do it myself."

# WHICH POTTY IS BEST?

### Choosing the Best Seat for Your Child

The best potty is both comfortable for your child and easy for you to clean. Choose a chair with a wide base that won't tip over and with handles for hanging on to during bowel movements. Make sure that your child's feet reach the floor or that he has some other support for his feet, so that he can push down during bowel movements. A sturdy, padded seat and a supportive back make longer potty sessions more comfortable, and a front tray for holding coloring books or toys makes them more fun. The fewer removable parts your child's potty has, the easier it will be to clean—an important consideration as toilet training proceeds.

To clean your child's potty, dump any waste into the adult toilet, thoroughly wipe the potty, and rinse it with water. You can also use some type of cleaning solution or disinfectant once a day.

On the other hand, children who are more focused on behaving like an older sibling may prefer using a stepstool to climb onto an adult toilet with a child's seat attached.

It isn't necessary to first put the potty in the bathroom. While some parents have found that placing the chair in the bathroom helps their child associate it more quickly with the

Though a potty is easiest for a young child to use, some families prefer to use a child-size seat attached to an adult toilet instead. Such seats may be preferable in small bathrooms, when the child will be using adult toilets due to travel or other activities and needs to get used to them, or when the child is strongly motivated to mimic adult bathroom use as closely as possible. Seats that attach to the toilet are preferable to inflatable seats that merely rest atop the adult seat, since the latter may feel unwieldy.

When toilet-training your child on an adult toilet, be prepared for resistance when it comes to flushing. Many children fear or dislike the flushing mechanism and the loud noise. Allow him the time and understanding he needs to overcome these feelings. But don't worry too much over the potty-versus-toilet issue. Children adapt eventually no matter where they're taught to eliminate, and a child's experiences of both potties and toilets combine to help her become fully toilet-trained.

act of elimination, others have met with greater success by keeping the potty in their child's bedroom, where it is easily accessible after a nap, or in the kitchen for use after meals. Later, when the child has begun to use the potty with some regularity, the potty can be moved to the bathroom or even replaced with a child's seat on an adult toilet.

## Getting to Know the Potty

As you may have discovered, the act of buying and installing a potty doesn't mean your child will use it. In most cases the association between the potty and elimination must be reinforced again and again before your child starts to catch on to the idea. Remind her frequently (but not so often that she begins to resist) that "this is where you can put your own poop and pee, just like Mommy does on her potty." Encourage her to spend time sitting on it while looking at books or playing with toys. Allow her to stay fully clothed at first if that's how she feels most comfortable. If you see your child squatting, getting red-faced, or otherwise signaling a need to have a bowel movement, suggest that she poop while sitting on the potty in her diaper. If she has a bowel movement in this way, you can then remove her diaper and let her "help" you move the stool from diaper to potty—thus strengthening the connection in her mind. Children who are in a "no-clothes" phase, quite common among toddlers and preschoolers, can sit naked on the potty and experience this association more directly.

### Dressing for the Potty

Once your child has grown comfortable with the idea of the potty and its associations with elimination have been reinforced, it's time to make it easier for her to use the potty successfully. Switch from diapers to underwear, involving your child in the process by allowing her to pick out her own underwear at the store. (Underpants decorated with favorite action figures or cartoon characters are popular.) If she has observed an older child using the bathroom in a particular kind of underwear, see if you can provide your toddler with underpants that look similar. It is surprising how literal some young children's ideas of bathroom use can be. Your child may initially believe that if she's not wearing underpants just like her brother's, she won't be able to use the potty.

---

### PARENT POTTY TIPS

### Making It Happen the First Time

In many cases, a child's first use of her potty is the most difficult. Here are some techniques that other parents have used to help their children toward their first successes.

**Run water in the sink** while your child is sitting on the potty. The sound of water may stimulate her voiding reflex.

**Provide an imaginary role model** and tell your child while he sits on the potty that "Superman pees into the potty, and so can you." Use any superhero, idol, or character that your child loves.

**Let your child read** while sitting on the potty. A good choice might be one of the many potty-training books for toddlers.

**Let her "demonstrate"** how a potty is used to another child, her favorite stuffed animal, or you. She is likely to imitate your own lessons perfectly and may even use the potty in the process.

**Stay with her** while she's on the potty or the toilet. She's more likely to sit still long enough to succeed if you're paying attention to her.

**Letting her do it her own way** is important so if your child likes to wear a special hat
while sitting on the potty, or wants to color
while she waits to urinate, let her do so. Sitting and waiting is boring; she'll feel better if
she has some control of the situation.

**Make it fun** and drop a few pieces of ce-
real or a few drops of food coloring into the
potty for your child to aim at. Playing games
takes the pressure off your child and makes
her want to "do it again."

**Try and relax.** The more positive and casual you are about the process, the easier it
will be for her to conform to your wishes.
Crack a few jokes to ease her wait on the
potty. She might laugh so hard that she succeeds by accident!

---

Your child's other clothes should also make it as easy as
possible to get into position on the potty in time. Avoid over-
alls, blue jeans, tights, or anything with zippers, buttons, or a
belt that she will have difficulty removing. Stick to short
dresses with panties for girls or elastic-waisted pants or shorts
for either sex—or allow your child to wear nothing below the
waist when at home if she prefers. Training pants, while
tempting to use since they absorb any accidents, are not ideal
for this period because they are hard for your child to pull
down. Training pants work well at night, absorbing any accidents until your child becomes night-trained.

## STANDING OR SITTING?

Parents often wonder whether to start training boys to urinate standing up or sitting down. While there is no definitive or "best" answer to this question, toddler boys are usually encouraged to sit down to urinate until they've grown familiar with the process of potty use and their aim while urinating is likely to have improved. By age two and a half or three, when children become interested in the concept of gender, boys begin to copy their fathers, friends, or older brothers and stand up when urinating. As your son learns to do this, make sure he lifts the toilet seat beforehand. Be prepared to do some extra cleaning around the toilet bowl for a while, since he probably won't have perfect aim for some time. (Make sure the toilet seat stays in the raised position when put there; injuries have been caused by falling seats.)

### Identifying Times to Go

Once your child is familiar with her potty, keep an eye out for opportunities to allow her to use it successfully. Ask her to tell you when she is about to urinate or have a bowel movement. At first she will be more likely to tell you about a wet diaper or bowel movement after the fact. In this case, praise her for telling you, and suggest that next time she let you know in advance.

You can also help your child become more aware of her elimination needs by reminding her after naptime and fifteen to twenty minutes after each meal. Whenever you see that she's about to defecate or urinate, point out that her grunting or squatting means it's time for the pee or poop to come out, and lead her toward the potty. The more independent you can help her feel during this step—allowing her to walk to the potty instead of carrying her, letting her pull down her own pants (with a little help from you, perhaps)—the more successful she will feel and the less likely she may be to resist.

Once your child is seated on the potty, ask her to try to poop or pee. If nothing happens, squat down next to her, hold her hand, chat with her, pick up one of her toys and use it to play with her, read her a story, or otherwise try to keep her seated happily on the potty for a while (but no longer than three to five minutes). If she becomes restless or resistant, however, let her go. Trying to force her to begin toilet training will only create more resistance and make the training process more difficult.

When your child finally does succeed in eliminating into the potty, reward her with praise, a hug, and a comment on what a big girl she's becoming. Tell others in the family about her success, and encourage them to praise her as well. Continue to praise your child each time she uses the potty or even makes an effort to do so—but don't overdo it or she'll feel pressured. In general, a light, positive "I knew you could do it!" attitude works best.

When an accident happens, treat it lightly and focus on reassuring your child while cleaning up.

### "What a Big Girl!": Following Up on Success

"My daughter, Tara, used her potty the very first day we brought it home," reports her mother, Anita. "I thought we had it made as far as toilet training went—but then she refused to go near the potty for the next two weeks. I already had her in underwear, so I spent the entire two weeks cleaning up after her accidents. That wasn't exactly what I had planned."

Your child's mastery of the potty, as with other developmental tasks, is a gradual progression, beginning with not being able to eliminate, continuing through being able to eliminate but not consistently, and finishing with total mastery. It should not come as a surprise when initial successes on the potty are followed by setbacks or regression.

While success on the potty is the most effective, reinforcing teaching tool available, the time it takes for this lesson to sink in varies widely. Some children adjust to potty use almost immediately and continue to use the potty with few accidents. Most, however, repeat their successes only sporadically for the first few days, weeks, or even months, gradually increasing potty use as they enjoy the parental praise and feelings of independence that accompany it.

After your child has successfully used the potty several times at your suggestion, try hanging back a bit to see if she will respond to the urge to use the potty on her own. It's all right to verbally prompt her occasionally—particularly at times when she usually needs to eliminate or if her behavior indicates she needs to go (dancing around, clutching her genital area, squatting). But don't constantly ask if she has to go to the bathroom, since that will rob her of her sense of control and cause her to resist.

When a mistake happens, treat it lightly and try not to get upset. Focus instead on keeping her meals and naps on a regular schedule, asking her after each naptime and meal if she needs to go, and feeding her plenty of fruits, other foods high in fiber, and liquids. This will make her body's urges more predictable and she will then be more likely to respond to them.

## OFFERING A REWARD

Parents sometimes worry that offering a child a tangible reward for using the potty, such as a small toy, is equivalent to bribing her to perform well. (They feel that a child should learn to perform for the sake of doing well, and that treats or other rewards distract from this learning process.) It is true that large rewards, such as a trip to her favorite pizza place or a major new toy, not only can be too expensive to provide for each bathroom success but also can encourage your child to focus on increasing the reward with each accomplishment instead of enjoying her success.

Praise and small rewards can be an effective way to demonstrate to your child in concrete ways that she has done well and should be pleased with her own behavior. You can also consider making a "potty chart" to which your child can add a gold star for each success. Whatever reward system you use, don't forget that hugs and praise are the most powerful motivators for your child. Because of the growing concern about obesity in children, it is better not to reward your child with food or candy.

When your child does respond to her urge by going to the potty, managing her clothes, and successfully eliminating, continue to praise her every time. Most parents find that adding potty use to a list of chores or achievements (such as laying out the napkins for dinner, feeding the fish, or brushing her teeth) and letting the child add a star or sticker next to each chore accomplished enhances her feelings of pride while placing toilet training in the proper context of just another life skill that must be mastered. With time, you can gradually phase out rewards as she accomplishes toilet training.

### Achieving Consistency

Some potty-training toddlers and preschoolers succeed with bowel movements before urination, because it is easier for them to delay a bowel movement long enough to get to

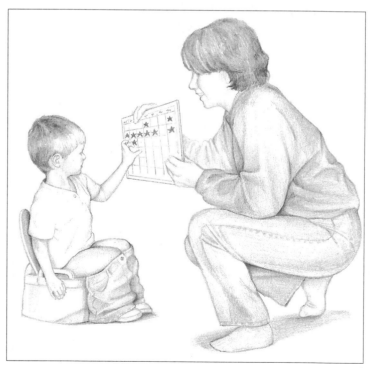

Small rewards, such as a sticker on a chart for each successful potty visit, can enhance a child's feeling of pride and motivate him to continue training.

the potty. Others begin urinating into a potty or toilet long before they are willing to defecate into one, though it may take longer for them to urinate consistently in the potty without frequent accidents. Whether your child achieves complete bowel or bladder control first, your job is to remain positive and supportive through their entire learning process.

While full daytime training may take a little longer than you had expected, your child will master this skill soon enough. Many parents comment that while such extended phases of training seem to last forever at the time, in retrospect they seem to end quite quickly. Refrain from returning to diapers if possible (this would most likely make your child feel as though he had failed), keep the pressure gentle but steady, and try to maintain a sense of humor until training is complete.

Keep in mind, too, that nighttime bladder control usually occurs later than daytime training. There's no harm in keeping your child in training pants or diapers at night until he has mastered daytime potty use.

## A PARENT'S STORY

### Prepare for, and Accept, Accidents

"Looking back on the toilet-training period with our daughter, Lizzy, I'd say the smartest thing we did was accept the fact that accidents were going to happen, and we needed to prepare for them ahead of time. We put a plastic sheet on the mattress. We even covered the car seat with plastic. We kept the necessary cleaning supplies on hand at home and when we went out. And we always took along a change of clothes wherever we took Lizzy. We still got a little frustrated a couple of times when she seemed to forget everything she'd learned, but minimizing the damage ahead of time made the process a lot easier."

Caroline, mother of Lizzy

## A PARENT'S STORY

### Musical Potty Chair

"Our pediatrician suggested that my two-year-old daughter pick out her own potty in hopes of sparking her interest in potty training. She selected a battery-powered potty that sang and lit up when the waste collection pan was filled. Day after day we encouraged her to 'be a big girl and use the potty.' Sometimes we were successful; other times she'd immediately spring off the potty after a few seconds. One evening I placed my daughter on the potty; obeying her request for privacy, I walked into the other room. After about twenty seconds I heard from behind the door, 'Yay! It's toilet paper time!' While clapping in excitement I pushed the door open to find my daughter, still sitting on the potty, spraying the sensor with a water bottle. She had figured out a way to activate the song without actually peeing on the potty. I stood in the doorway of the bathroom in complete shock, not sure if I was mad that she had tricked me into thinking that she had used the potty or proud that she had the intelligence and curiosity to figure out how the potty 'really' worked."

Diamond, mother of Stella

## Moving On: Increasing Confidence and Self-Esteem

Toilet training is an uneven process, but it is an inevitable one in nearly every child's life. By three to four years of age, most children have achieved daytime urine control and full bowel control (both day and night). The ability to stay dry through the night will follow a bit later, with most girls and more than 75 percent of boys fully mastering this ability by around age six.

Your child, too, will move more or less steadily from diapers to underwear, from potty to toilet, and from daytime to full-time management of his elimination processes. Many parents find, in fact, that once their child grasps the concept of one form of elimination, mastery in the other areas follows with greater ease (yet still on its own schedule). Soon your child will announce confidently in restaurants and airports that he needs to find a bathroom, will lead you by the hand to the restroom, and will confidently use a toilet he's never seen before.

In the meantime, your continued support and sensitivity to his needs will encourage his progress. As he moves from a potty to the adult toilet at home, provide him with a stepstool if he needs it and a child-size toilet seat. (The age at which this transition occurs will depend on your child's interest, your needs, and environmental requirements such as the need to use adult-style toilets more frequently outside the home.)

When your child needs to use the toilet away from home, accompany and assist him, making sure that he follows the same routine (wipe, flush, wash hands) that he has learned at home. Consider bringing his potty or a child's toilet seat adapter along on trips, as well as a change of clothing. It may also help to allow your child to observe you using the toilet in these unfamiliar places, and talk to him about what a big boy he will be when he can do the same. Before he starts school, make sure he can pull his pants up and down properly. (See Chapter 6 for more information on supporting your child's toilet use away from home.)

Such efforts to support your child will increase his confidence in bathroom use, but they will do much more than that. They will let him know in many important ways how committed you are to helping him learn new skills and adjust to new challenges. By allowing him to develop at his own rate, withholding criticism or judgment when he fails, and offering praise when he succeeds, you have shown him that he can set a goal for himself and achieve it.

By continuing to teach him how to manage his personal functions the way big kids and adults do, you are helping him achieve his greatest goal—increased independence and self-mastery. In many ways, toilet-training success is not only a demonstration of all that your child has learned in a few short years of life but also an indication of how he will overcome challenges and meet goals in the years to come.

## Q & A

### Is He Okay?

**Q:**    My son, who was recently toilet-trained, often goes two or three days in a row without a bowel movement. Is this normal, or might he be withholding stool?

**A:**    The frequency of children's bowel movements varies widely, and it can be difficult for parents to know what is normal. Some children move their bowels two or three times a day, while others may go two or three days between movements. In general, a marked change in your child's stooling pattern is more important to note. If you notice such a change or if your child becomes uncomfortable, talk with your pediatrician. Do not give your child laxatives, suppositories, stool softeners, or enemas unless your pediatrician recommends them. A well-balanced diet with plenty of fruit, fiber, and liquids (preferably water) is the best way to create soft, comfortable stools and regular bowel movements.

**Q:** My one-year-old shadow follows me to the bathroom every time I go, and stares at me while I use the toilet. Her attention is embarrassing. Is it okay not to allow this to happen?

**A:** Of course you don't have to use the bathroom in your child's presence, but observing a parent (especially a same-sex parent) using the toilet is one of the best ways to teach her how to do the same. Not only does observation answer a lot of your toddler's unvoiced questions about elimination, but soon the desire to mimic your behavior may spur her to actually ask to use the toilet and to switch from diapers to underwear. Continue allowing her to observe you if you can avoid feeling too uncomfortable. If you feel, however, that your embarrassment is having a negative effect on your child, once she is old enough and ready to use the potty, consider having her observe another willing family member, or look to other methods (conversation, children's books, direct instruction) to familiarize her with the process.

**Q:**    My daughter has been successfully potty-trained during the day. However, she is four and a half and still has accidents at night. I hear similar stories from other parents. Some suggest waiting for her to get older, while others say to try incentives for her to stay dry at night. But I am not sure she has much control over it.

**A:**    Stay positive! Bedwetting is quite common through five years of age and can continue through eight to ten years of age, particularly if there is a family history of bedwetting. Chapter 4 offers insight into why accidents may happen during the night, as well as during the potty-training process. Being prepared in advance will help you react with the appropriate response, and help you and your child continue the training when she is ready.

CHAPTER 4

# ACCIDENTS, RESISTANCE, AND OTHER TOILET-TRAINING CHALLENGES

No one expects a child to be perfect. Problems and challenges with toilet training can occur at any point in the process. Often they are temporary, but they can persist. Many parents find their children's bathroom-related accidents particularly frustrating.

One reason for this, of course, is the unpleasant process of cleaning up afterward. Another is the fact that accidents are more likely to occur when parents are feeling rushed, the family is stressed, or the child is in an unfamiliar environment—just those times when mistakes can be most upsetting. But sometimes issues of shame, control, and one's self-image as a parent become part of the equation as well, increasing the emotional impact of the accident beyond that of other everyday mishaps, and beyond what it should be.

PARENT POTTY TIPS

**Be Prepared**

For at least six months after toilet training is complete, when you go on outings continue to bring along diaper wipes, a change of clothes, and any other supplies you might require in case of an accident. Make sure there's time for a bathroom visit before you leave the house, and be aware that chances of a mishap are greater when your child finds herself in unfamiliar surroundings.

To help your child prevent such accidents, be on the lookout for public bathrooms, and when you see one ask her if she has to go. Teach her to look for and recognize the men's and women's symbols on public restroom doors. At home, keep plastic liners under your child's bedsheets in case of unexpected bedwettings and continue to keep cleaning supplies near at hand. The more prepared you are for accidents, the easier it will be to clean up and not make your child feel bad about her accident.

Yet the fact remains that bathroom accidents are nearly always just that—accidents resulting from forgetfulness, momentary distraction, or waiting too long before trying to get to a bathroom. By responding calmly to this behavior as a normal and understandable part of learning a new skill, you can prevent the power struggles, avoidance, anxiety, rebellion, and other emotional entanglements that may perpetuate toilet-training problems.

## "Again?": Why Accidents Happen

The childcare center Stephanie was attending for the first time was enormous—like an indoor playground with children of different ages running around her in all directions. Stephanie's mother had shown her around the room and introduced her to the caregivers before she left, but that seemed a very long time ago, and now Stephanie was all alone. She stood near the wooden sink in the play kitchen, gazing in awe at the unfamiliar plastic dishes, the painted burner on the toy stove, and the bowl full of plastic fruit. Nearby, two boys were fighting for control of a toy train set, and one boy hit the other on the head with the train engine. The noise of the second boy's crying filled Stephanie's head, increasing her confusion and anxiety. She looked around for a grown-up. There was a lady across the room. *Help!* Stephanie thought, but did not know enough to say. *That noise is so loud!*

Suddenly Stephanie felt a warm, wet sensation on her inner thighs beneath her jeans. She looked down. *Uh-oh. An accident.* Vague, undefined feelings of disappointment and shame filled her, crowding out all thoughts of her surroundings. Unable to think of how to fix the situation, Stephanie started to cry. Then, a moment later, a grown-up's arms were around her shoulders and a friendly voice murmured, "Hey, Stephanie, it's okay. You had an accident. We'll dry you off and put some clean clothes on you right away."

We adults sometimes forget how intensely young children experience their world, and how easily thrown they are by any change in their daily routine or their surroundings. At ages two, three, and four, toddlers or preschoolers have come so far in terms of verbal skills and general comprehension that it's easy to overestimate their ability to focus, prioritize, and remember. Research has shown, however, that through the entire toddler and preschool period children remain weak in their ability to select and prioritize information from the flood of sensations that reaches them. A young child walking along the sidewalk with a parent is as likely to focus on the sounds of birdsong in the trees as on her parent's voice or the car speeding past a few feet away.

A child who finds herself struggling to cope with a wide variety of stimuli in an unfamiliar environment, as Stephanie did in the example above, may easily miss her body signaling the need to eliminate. Even when a toddler is just headed for the bathroom in her own home, she may be sufficiently distracted by the sound of a whistling teapot in the kitchen to forget where she is going.

Parents frequently find that bathroom accidents are more common when their toddlers and preschoolers are playing outside, watching television, playing on the computer, painting pictures, or otherwise focusing so intently on one activity that they fail to notice their physical needs and signals. An inner focus on another aspect of development—acquiring a new skill or coping with an emotional issue—can have the same effect. Another factor to take into account is that young children's memories tend to be more situation-specific than most adults realize. Your child may use her potty every day without mishap at home but "forget" the necessary sequence of actions at a friend's house or restaurant, on a day when her ordinary routine has been altered, or even when she is wearing tights or some other new variation on her usual clothes. Young children also have difficulty thinking ahead of time about their bathroom needs and must be reminded to use the potty before going out even though they don't urgently need to.

---

### PARENT POTTY TIPS

### The Right Response

What's the best way to respond when a child who is toilet-trained has an "accident"?

Your response depends on the age of your child and where he is in regard to his toilet training. It is best to first determine the likely cause for your child's accident, such as being too distracted by other activities or not feeling comfortable on the toilet. Being able to correct the cause, particularly in young children, is likely to work better than you trying to explain it. Then, if he is old enough to understand, you can express mild regret, help your child see what he should have done instead, and clean up and move on.

Here are some tips from other parents on how to keep bathroom accidents from becoming a larger issue than they should be:

**Don't pretend that "it's okay."** While it's not a good idea to yell at a child who has wet her pants as it will only increase her anxiety around this issue and may cause her to have even more accidents in the future, it is important for your child to understand that it is not acceptable to urinate or defecate wherever she likes. A simple "Oh, too bad. I know you wanted to use the potty. It feels yucky to be all wet" will do. Then move quickly toward getting her clean and dry. For older children (over four years of age) you may want to briefly explain what she could have done differently in this situation.

**Be concrete.** Don't tell your child, "You should tell me sooner when you need to go." Instead, press gently on her lower abdomen and tell her, "The first time you feel that funny feeling right here that means you have to go, tell a grown-up and they'll take you to a bathroom right away." If you observe that your child has some fears, such as flushing the toilet, it may help to work through her fear, such as by sprinkling bits of paper into the toilet, asking her to flush it, and then holding her hand and explaining what's happening as the paper goes away. Rather than complain about having to clean up after an accident, have your child hand you the toilet paper or paper towels and watch you deposit stool in the potty, where it belongs.

If your child will be spending time in a new place, such as a childcare center or preschool, take her to the bathroom and encourage her to try using the toilet. Such physical experiences go a long way in helping children retain mastery of a new skill. In each new environment, Mom or Dad may want to use the bathroom themselves in order to model what they want the child to

do, and continue to use bathrooms in loca-
tions away from home until the child is fully
toilet-trained.

Finally, despite the leaps your child may have taken in
verbal ability over the past two or three years, new situations
or experiences may still leave him at a loss for words. He may
not know how to tell you that his skin is irritated, causing
pain when he urinates, or that he's constipated and it hurts to
poop. It is helpful to keep track of how frequently he has a
bowel movement (so that you can notice if he is having a
movement less often than once every two days), and to notice
if he is having hard bowel movements or if he is straining to
move his bowels. If your child experiences any of the above,
you probably should speak with your child's pediatrician
to consider possible causes. She may recommend dietary
changes and/or stool softeners. If moving his bowels is uncomfortable, your child can get into a vicious cycle where
holding back as long as possible can make the actual movement more difficult and or painful.

All of these behaviors are perfectly normal and age-
appropriate for your child. In fact, as suggested earlier, it is a
good rule of thumb to wait at least six months after your
child starts using the potty to consider him fully trained. By
praising him for his progress and teaching him to think
ahead, focus, and plan better regarding toilet use, but continuing to keep cleanup aids at hand, you allow him to continue learning at the pace that is appropriate for his age, to
experiment with variations on his original routine, and to
discard behaviors that clearly don't work.

Like you, he will have good days and bad days in terms of
focus, memory, and performance in all aspects of his behav-

ior. Like you, he will progress more smoothly and quickly in response to praise and patience—along with firm and consistent instruction—than to harsh criticism or ridicule.

### Active Resistance

Accidents become a more serious issue when they become part of a power struggle between parent and child. This occurs most often when a conflict exists between the parent's approach to toilet training and the child's temperament, stage of development, or learning style.

A parent who constantly asks her child if he needs to go, for example, may spark resistance in the child if he is in an independent phase. In an attempt to control his own routine, the child may refuse to admit he needs to use the potty until it's too late and he has an accident. Another child who tends to daydream and is easily distracted may experience an increase in accidents because his parents don't remind him to go and he forgets to. A shy child may avoid using a potty that has been placed in the family room for the sake of convenience even though this strategy worked well for her gregarious older sisters, while a sociable toddler may avoid the toilet if his parents routinely shut the bathroom door. Physically active children often start to resist the toilet-training routine if they are made to sit on the potty for more than three to five minutes at a time.

At first such accidents are no more problematic than the incidental mishaps described earlier in this chapter. But when parents fail to change their approach to alleviate the child's problem, or react too emotionally or negatively to his mistakes, the child is likely to resist even more. This resistance can create more frustration and even anger on the part of the parents, whose increasingly negative responses lead to more resistance and outright rebellion in an ever-escalating cycle. Some children may even hold in their bowel movements to the point where they become constipated. This may create a vicious cycle where the constipation makes it even harder and more uncomfortable for him to move his bowels.

It is best to resolve such issues as early as possible, preferably before they turn into full-blown power struggles. If your child's accidents have started to increase during the training process, or if you sense for any other reason that he is resisting your training efforts, your first response should be to back off a bit and let him set the pace for a few weeks, thus breaking the cycle of resistance. Use this time to "play detective," observing his bathroom behavior to try to determine what it is about the training process that hasn't been working for him.

For instance, does he keep the door open or closed when he uses the potty? Does he like to talk about potty use, or does he avoid such conversations? Does he linger so long at his games or activities that he has an accident? Does he leap off the potty just before he urinates, unable to sit still long enough to succeed? Now that you are not frequently reminding him to use the potty, does he have accidents less often—or more?

Once you have an idea about the most common causes of your child's accidents, consider whether your own behavior helps or hinders the situation. If your child is old enough and his verbal skills are sufficiently developed, you might even talk with him about these issues. A child who feels very private about potty use may appreciate your offer to respect his feelings—perhaps to use an agreed-on secret signal to alert him that it may be time to use the potty rather than a loud "Andrew, do you need to go?" A child who's easily distracted may respond with relief to a reliable potty routine based on predictable, easy-to-remember sessions—potty after break-fast, after naptime, after lunch.

A child whose memory is still very situation-specific may benefit from "what-if" conversations—for example, "What if you're at a friend's house and you don't know where the bathroom is?" Sometimes all it takes to decrease resistance is to

## WHY KIDS RESIST

Children are often unable to explain the problems they have with our parenting techniques, and your child's only option may be to resist your effort to toilet-train her. When trying to discern the reasons behind her resistance, it may help to quickly review the following common causes:

- **Physical pain** caused by infection or constipation
- **Confusion** about the toilet-training process or about what is expected of her
- **Curiosity** about what will happen if she resists
- **Anxiety or fear** about the process of elimination, or fear of the potty or toilet
- **Independence and control issues** that make it hard for her to satisfy your wishes at this time
- **Too much pressure** to perform
- **Inappropriate toilet-training technique** that does not suit her personality or learning style

accept your child's quirks of personality (wanting to run the water in the bathroom sink while he urinates, refusing to poop unless all his clothes are off) and temperament (enjoying long sessions on the potty without using it, wanting someone to talk to while he goes) instead of trying to make him adapt to standard practice or the approach you've used with his siblings. As your child realizes that you are accepting of and willing to respond to his particular needs, he will become much more responsive to your toilet-training efforts.

*Transitions and Disruptions* Changes in your child's daily routine can lead to resistance. A new sibling or caregiver, guests staying in your home, a change in your own schedule leading to less time spent parenting, or virtually any other type of transition or disruption can create anxiety that leads to a decrease in your child's willingness or ability to stick to bathroom routines. He may be too self-conscious to admit to a new caregiver that he needs to use the potty, and have an accident instead. The presence of overnight guests may confuse or frighten him, causing him to put a stop to toilet-training efforts. He may feel lonely or abandoned to some degree as you focus on a new job or other activity, and resist training as a way of getting your attention. You may be able to avoid some of this type of resistance by preparing your child as fully as possible for any disruption that you know is coming.

The more concretely you can do this—by introducing him to the new caregiver ahead of time and talking with the two of them about his potty-training routines, showing him photographs of the household guests and discussing how he will use the bathroom while they're visiting, playing a favorite game with him and promising to do so regularly even after your new job begins, and so on—the less disoriented he may feel when the change actually occurs. If he still responds by resisting potty use, understand that this is a normal response, talk with him about the cause of his distress, take active steps to help him adjust, ask others around him to be mindful of the anxiety he is feeling, and remain patient as he gradually relaxes enough to take up his potty-training efforts again.

While it's clearly best to postpone potty training if you know a transition is about to occur, even unexpected changes can usually be managed easily. Accidents will probably increase in number for a few days, or even a few weeks, but resistance will soon fade as you offer added support and your child becomes comfortable with the new status quo.

*Infections and Irritations* One cause of resistance to potty training that parents may overlook at first is a physical or medical problem. By noting how frequently your child poops and gently asking him whether it hurts to pee or poop, you may find that skin irritation in the genital or anal area, a urinary tract infection, or constipation is the cause of his mishaps; if so, you can remedy the situation before it gets worse. Discuss your observations with your child's pediatrician, and see Chapter 6 for more information on these and other common medical problems.

---

### PARENT POTTY TIPS

#### Stay Positive

You wouldn't perform better on the job if your boss yelled at you each time you made a mistake. Your child will meet your expectations more easily if she sees that you believe she can and will do so.

**Relax.** Toilet training is your child's challenge, not yours. Refrain from constantly asking her if she needs to go. Let her learn to recognize her own body's signs and respond to them appropriately. Sometimes a little inattention on your part will lead to a little more effort on hers.

**Remember, it's not forever.** If you find yourself getting upset over an accident with your toilet-trained child, fix a date six months from now in your mind. Assure yourself that by that date your child will probably no longer have daytime accidents (though there may be exceptions now and then for years to come). By remembering how short this hit-and-miss period really is, you can temper your reaction to minor setbacks.

---

*Moving Too Fast* It is a good idea to consider the possibility that, despite initial appearances, your child isn't ready to complete toilet training, and is trying to tell you this in the only way he knows how. If efforts to adapt your technique to his needs have led to no improvement, and medical issues and changes in his environment have been ruled out, think about putting a hold on potty training for a few weeks. During that time, observe how your child responds. If he has a number of accidents per day and you find this especially upsetting, you might consider offering to provide him with diapers or training pants again until he's ready to resume his potty-training efforts.

If possible, though, it's best to avoid backtracking in this way, since he is likely to experience a return to diapers as a setback in his growth and feel even less motivated to use the potty. Instead, focus on helping him relearn positive behaviors more efficiently by keeping his clothing easy to remove, his potty chair convenient, and your praise and other rewards ever ready. If you can tolerate lack of progress for a while, your child may eventually "catch up" with himself and resume training as though nothing had happened.

## Two Steps Back: Regression

One parent recently explained, "Our daughter made great progress with toilet training the first two weeks. But when she started at the new childcare center, it was like she forgot everything she'd learned. She never told the adults in charge when she needed to go. She had one or two accidents a day at the center, and even had them at home on the weekends. When we tried to talk to her about it, she would just look at us like she had no idea what we were talking about, or would run away and play."

We adults are accustomed to acquiring new skills at a steady pace and retaining what we learn. Young children, however, whose learning often depends on their development in other areas, frequently progress in a series of sudden spurts interspersed with periods of little apparent improvement. At times a child may even regress in her learning—that is, lose skills she has recently acquired or even take a few steps back in her learning process.

Regression during toilet training—a child's sudden neglect of potty practices, constant "puddling" or other accidents, or desire to return to diapers—can be baffling and upsetting to parents who believe they have nearly completed the process. Your first response to such behavior in your child is to have her examined by her pediatrician to be sure the cause is not physical. As you will learn in Chapter 6, regression sometimes signals an infection or other disorder that requires medical treatment. If medical causes have been ruled out, however, your child is probably simply responding in the only way she knows how to a recent change in her environment or some other source of stress in her life.

Common causes of regression in young children include:

- Change in the childcare routine—for example, a new sitter, or starting a childcare or preschool program
- The mother's pregnancy or the birth of a new sibling
- A major illness on the part of the child or a family member
- A recent death
- Parents' marital conflict or divorce
- An upcoming or recent move to a new house
- Constipation/painful bowel movements
- Urinary tract infection
- Other medical problems

Such events—even when they are happy ones—can represent a real challenge to young children still struggling to master their own personal routines. Just as you may choose to drop your diet or exercise routine during a difficult period at work, your child may need to take some time off from toilet training to adjust to her new home situation. Far from signaling an emotional problem, regression can actually be a healthy way for a child to meet her emotional needs at a time when life feels overwhelming.

In Chapter 6 you will find more information about some of the emotional issues that can lead to regression. For now, when responding to regressive behavior during the training process, focus on taking the following steps to help get your child back on track.

The best solution for cases of regression is to identify the cause of the backsliding (such as a move to a new house), offer empathy and support, and take practical steps toward returning to better habits.

• **Identify the problem.** Is there a good reason for the regression, such as a new sibling or other change in her environment? As verbal as your toddler or preschooler may be, it is frequently not possible for children this age to understand or express what they are feeling. If there is not a readily observable reason, you should contact your pediatrician to determine if there is a more physical reason, such as constipation. Let your child know that you've noticed her change in behavior—that she has stopped using her potty, has been having a lot of accidents at the childcare center, or has been talking about wearing diapers again. Ask her why this might be—because her potty is in a new bathroom in your new house now, because the toilet at the childcare center is scary, or because her new baby brother wears a diaper and he has been getting so much attention lately? Listen to her response, and help her try to communicate the actual events that are upsetting her as well as her feelings about them, although your child may not be aware or able to verbalize that she has regressed.

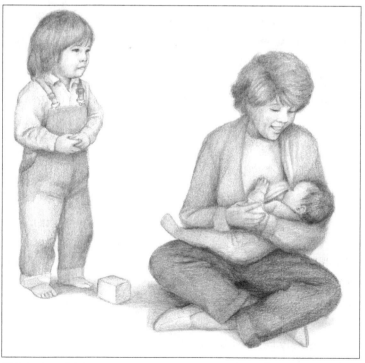

Although a child may regress in situations such as the arrival of a new sibling, regression usually ends when the child retrains herself after a few days or weeks.

- **Do what you can to fix the problem.** If there are practical steps you can take to ease your child's distress, do so as soon as possible. Arrange for a special time to spend alone with your child (without her baby brother), accompany her to the childcare center to talk with the caregivers about how they can help your child maintain her bathroom habits, or surround her potty in the new house with familiar objects from the old house. Ask your child to contribute ideas, too, on how to improve her situation. By helping her to "own" her problem and its resolution in this way, you will commit her to a more active role in correcting it.

- **Be clear about your expectations.** Particularly for younger children, these expectations are to a great extent nonverbal, such as having the potty readily available and sitting her on the potty at times you think she's more likely to go. For the older child, let her know that you are fully confident that she will achieve success and pee on the potty. Support her with positive reinforcements, including hugs and praise, stickers on a chart, and an occasional pep talk as she struggles to regain her footing.

If your child's regression stretches on for a month or more, you may need to ask yourself whether she was ready to be fully day-trained in the first place. There's no harm in suggesting that you set the potty aside for a while if it's clear that this would be a big relief to your child. But this is an exception to the general rule that moving forward, however gradually, is usually best. Upsetting as regression can be to parents, it usually doesn't last very long. In many cases, the child picks up where she left off in toilet training after a few days or weeks.

# FROM THE EXPERTS

### Anticipate, but Don't Assume

"In my experience as a child psychologist, I have occasionally seen parents worry too much about how a major life change will affect their child. One mother I observed actually stopped in the middle of toilet-training her son when she learned that the family would be moving in a couple of months. While it's true that her son might have regressed somewhat just before or after the move, chances are he would not have. Meanwhile, the mother interrupted what had been good progress at a time when her son was ready to learn this new skill.

"I advise parents to continue toilet training until they see that their child really is too stressed out to deal with it. If he does regress, they can support him through the transition. But by continuing the training process while talking with their child about the upcoming change and helping him adjust to a new routine or environment, they can often not only complete training without interruption but also help the child learn how resilient and capable he is."

Dr. Maureen O'Brien, psychologist

## Different Skills, Different Schedules

One of the most difficult aspects of toilet training for many parents is the uneven pace at which different types of training occur. Your child may learn to urinate into a potty quite easily but take several more months to start having bowel movements there. Daytime training may have been a breeze for your toddler, but he continues to wet the bed frequently through age five or even older. Since the order and speed with which each of these skills is mastered may differ from child to child, it is impossible to compare one child's mastery with another's to determine whether your child's progress is "normal." In most cases, the best response to uneven adoption of skills is to remain patient and supportive, giving your child the time he needs to take the next step toward complete success.

Delays in bowel control can be particularly disturbing for many parents, however—especially when children exhibit such puzzling behavior as secretly depositing bowel movements in a closet or other hiding place, smearing feces on the wall or other surface, or bursting into tears when their stool is flushed down the toilet. Our own adult associations with bowel movements are so negative that it is hard to remember that very young children have little awareness of the presence of germs, the potential for mess, the attached cultural stigma, and so on. On the contrary, toddlers and preschoolers are often extremely proud of the products their bodies have created—expecting praise and admiration, not displeasure—and are reluctant or even anxious at the prospect of letting these products go. This reluctance can grow even stronger during periods when mastery of their body or privacy becomes a high-priority issue in

# A PARENT'S STORY

### "My Body!"

"My son, Trevor, was easy to toilet-train as far as urination went, but he refused to do number two into his potty or the toilet. Lots of times he just pooped in his underwear. Then for a while, there wasn't any poop at all. I finally found out that he had picked a place behind the shrubs in the backyard to deposit his stool. He had it out there on a pile of leaves. But when I asked him about it, all he could tell me was that it was his poop and he wasn't going to let it go.

"I decided not to do anything with it except cover it up with dirt and leaves. It seemed he didn't want to let go of his stool when he was sitting on the potty. I guess he thought of it as a part of his body, and I think he didn't like feeling it fall away and hearing it hit the bowl. So what I did was, I stuffed a diaper inside the potty bowl and let him poop into the diaper. Then, gradually, I cut away at the diaper until it was a small square of cloth. Finally, shortly after lunch on a day when I'd made sure he'd had some fruit juice and fiber, I talked him into sitting on the potty without the cloth. Pretty soon he pooped—and it wasn't so bad! I let him empty it into the toilet and flush it away himself. After that, he used the potty as if it had never been a problem."

Helen, mother of Trevor

their lives, or when they are experiencing a fear of the potty or of some other aspect of bowel training that they are unable to articulate.

While nighttime bowel control occurs quite early and naturally in most children, nighttime bladder control usually occurs much later—frequently months or even years after daytime training is complete. Forty percent of children in the United States continue to wet the bed while sleeping after they have been fully day-trained. Bedwetting continues to be quite common through age five; by age six you may want to check with your pediatrician. Many children under age six are not physiologically capable of remaining dry at night, since their bladders have not sufficiently matured and their bodies may not yet consistently wake them from sleep when it's time to urinate. Nearly every child will experience at least a few nighttime bedwettings before the toilet-training process is truly complete.

In Chapter 8 you will find a great deal of information on handling nighttime accidents and moving toward an end to bedwetting. In the meantime, since conflicts over such mishaps can easily spill over to cause resistance during the day, it is usually best to downplay any interventions through the toddler and even perhaps the preschool years. Beyond six years of age, you may want to discuss the issue with your pediatrician, who can check if there is a physical cause and help you set up a reward system such as a star chart or can recommend using an alarm system.

## An Early Exercise in Teamwork

Setbacks in toilet training are no fun for parent or child. It is difficult confronting even minor failures in children on whom we've pinned so many expectations, and bathroom use can be an especially touchy subject for some. Acknowledging and conquering the reasons behind setbacks can, however, turn out to be one of the most positive experiences you will have with your very young child. There is nothing

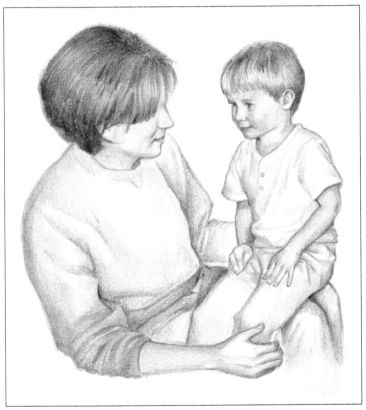

Staying positive when accidents happen and helping encourage your child through the ups and downs can help make for a smoother transition from diaper to potty.

like knowing that the two of you have met challenges and succeeded in the past to help you face new challenges in the future.

As you support your child during this aspect of self-mastery, make an effort to view this experience in light of your wider goals. Focus on helping your toddler or preschooler see that with effort she can triumph. Remember that young children want more than anything to learn and grow. Help yours to earn and enjoy the universal childhood boast, "See what a big kid I am!"

## Q & A

### Surviving the Setbacks

**Q:** I got upset at my three-year-old for having so many accidents, and now he withholds his stool for four or five days at a time. What should I do?

**A:** First, observe your child and his environment. Are there stressors in his environment that could be contributing to his behavior? Does he appear to be uncomfortable or scared when he is having a bowel movement? Meanwhile, be sure there is sufficient fruit and other foods high in fiber in his diet, and make sure he drinks lots of water to keep his stool soft. Consult your pediatrician if his toilet use does not normalize.

**Q:** My son is very regular in his bathroom habits, but I have one problem with him: he insists on pooping standing up. I have finally persuaded him to stand over his potty instead of in the bathtub, as he used to do, but he still refuses to sit down. What can I do about this?

**A:** Standing up for a bowel movement is a common habit for children who were used to defecating in their diaper while standing. Trying to poop while sitting probably feels unnatural and uncomfortable for your child. You have already started to solve this problem by persuading him to leave the bathtub, where he could stand and feel most comfortable, to the potty, where the stools belong. Next, suggest that he sit to urinate and then continue to sit until just an instant before he needs to poop, and reward him for his effort. It can also be helpful to be able to see his father or older brother poop sitting on the toilet. If he seems bothered by the potty, you can have him first learn to poop in his diaper sitting somewhere other than the potty. Continue to encourage him this way—particularly about fifteen minutes after meals and before bedtime, when the urge to have a bowel movement is greatest—until he accidentally releases stool into the potty while sitting. Reward him greatly for this success. Soon your reward system and your support will ease him into correct behavior.

**Q:** What can I do when my child refuses to use the bathroom before we leave the house?

**A:** Your child is expressing a desire to control her bathroom use, no matter what. Your best response is to allow her to experience the consequences of her actions. If she is already regularly using a potty or the toilet, she will not enjoy the accident that occurs while on the road. By packing cleaning supplies and a change of clothes (and covering the car seat with plastic if necessary), you will have made learning through experience as painless as possible for both of you while avoiding the extended problems a power struggle would cause.

## CHAPTER 5

# TOILET TRAINING AND THE OLDER CHILD

"My husband likes to tease me by calling my parenting style the 'lazy parent's method for raising a child,'" writes one mother. "I like to just wait for my son to move on to the next stage of development and then follow his lead. He toilet-trained himself when he was four because he wanted to—not because I decided it was time."

Such a relaxed attitude toward toilet training has grown somewhat more common in this country in recent years, though many parents continue to report surprised reactions from others who learn that their preschool-age children are still in diapers.

If your child has recently tried and failed to master the toilet-training process, or if he has never responded to your attempts to begin, it's a good idea to schedule a checkup with his pediatrician before beginning training. An examination can identify such common, treatable obstacles to toilet training as a bladder infection or bowel problems, particularly constipation. Your pediatrician can also explain how to compensate for physical or mental disabilities or developmental challenges. (See Chapters 6 and 7 for discussions of these issues.) Whether a physical issue or other problem is confirmed or ruled out, a visit to the pediatrician will give you a better understanding of how to work with your child, and it will help you and your child proceed with greater confidence.

## REASONS FOR DELAYED TOILET TRAINING

Here are some of the more common explanations from parents for why toilet training in their older child (age three and a half and up) has been delayed:

- They may have decided to delay training until their child expressed an interest.
- They may have attempted toilet training at an earlier time, only to give up when they met with resistance from the child.
- The child may have been fully trained but then regressed when a new sibling arrived or another major change occurred, causing the child never to return to his toilet-using routine.
- Their toddler or preschooler may have experienced physical or developmental challenges that interfered with bladder or bowel control.

Toilet-training a healthy older child can offer some advantages over training a toddler. For example, preschoolers may have an improved ability to visualize a goal and achieve it, as well as increased skill at communicating any confusion, anxiety, or resentment they may feel. An older child may also be more aware of other children's behavior, which can work to promote a smoother and faster transition.

Yet these same developments can also present new challenges. A child's ability to act on his own can spur his resistance to a parent's directions. A preschooler's improved verbal skills allow him to argue and negotiate. His awareness of other children's behavior may backfire if he feels ashamed of his continued diaper use. The simple force of a long-lived habit can also make it more difficult to achieve the transition out of diapers.

In most cases, parents find that toilet-training an older child is neither easier nor more difficult than training a toddler—just different. In this chapter we will explore the unique challenges and opportunities you are likely to experience with your preschooler or older child. We will also discuss ways to approach this developmental milestone in the most appropriate ways.

## "It's Your Body": Fostering Self-Management

Young children are generally eager to learn and grow, and will move naturally toward new stages of development with the support of the adults in their environment. Parents can best help children between the ages of three and five by providing the memory cues necessary to learn a new skill, while still allowing for the strong urge to "do it myself." Your four-year-old may resist being placed physically on the potty—

## A PARENT'S STORY

### My Independent Daughter

"My little girl, Francesca, has always been strong-willed. I tried to potty-train her several times during toddlerhood, but she refused to stop wearing diapers. By the time she was three, most of her friends had been toilet-trained, but she didn't seem to care. I really started to worry when she still showed no interest at age four.

"Then my sister, Mary, came to visit for a couple of weeks. Francesca just loved her and followed her everywhere. Mary decided to take advantage of the situation, talking to Francesca about potty use and letting my daughter follow her into the bathroom when she needed to go. Within a few days, Francesca had decided that she wanted to use the toilet 'just like Aunt Mary.' She didn't even use the potty, but climbed up onto the adult toilet. By the end of Mary's visit, Francesca had almost completely trained herself. I guess for a kid like her, it really is best to be patient and let her progress in her own way."

Eleanor, mother of Francesca

for example, a technique that works well for many younger toddlers—but he may respond to a verbal reminder ("Lunch

is over. Now, what's next?") that offers him a chance to respond successfully ("Potty time!") and go to the bathroom on
his own. By helping your child picture what she wants to do,
plan how to accomplish her goal, and carry through successfully, you can allow her to teach herself to use the potty. In
the process, she will learn that she can achieve the goals she
sets for herself, and her self-confidence will increase accordingly.

### Offering Suggestions

"I remember when I first learned to use a potty," one parent said (not entirely truthfully) to her attentive daughter. "I
didn't know how to do it at first. But my mom helped me
remember when it was time to go and she showed me where
the potty was. She let me put a bit of toilet paper in the potty
and try to get it wet with my pee. It was fun. Do you want to
try?"

Preschoolers love to hear stories about their parents. Talking to your child in a personal way about bathroom use is a
good way to support her both cognitively and emotionally. By
reassuring her that you've been there, too, and reviewing the
steps you took to learn to use the potty, you demonstrate that
she will be able to achieve her goals also. Whether you tell
your child a similar story or just suggest a straightforward
plan of action for beginning toilet training ("How about wearing that pretty princess underwear today? Don't worry about
getting it wet. We'll pay attention to when you need to pee
and I'll help you get to the bathroom in time"), your child
will welcome your help in laying out the steps she needs to
follow.

Once you have created a game plan with your child, it is

important to follow through consistently. You may have re-
marked to her, for example, that you usually need to use the
bathroom after meals and before bedtime, and the two of you
have agreed that she will try that, too. If so, be ready to remind her to sit on the potty at each of these times if necessary
and accompany her there if she is hesitant to go. You may
need to exert a little pressure to get her to stick to a plan that

Show your confidence in your child's ability to master toilet training by
giving him "grown-up" underwear.

she's agreed to. Refusing a reward until she's completed this
chore demonstrates that this responsibility must be met—
just like brushing her teeth and taking a bath.

Since your goal is to help your child move from being
reminded to use the potty toward recognizing and addressing the need on her own, it makes sense to support her
efforts further by offering helpful tips along the way. Just
as you would with a younger child, teach her to be aware of

# IS YOUR CHILD RELUCTANT?

Many children—even three- and four-year-olds—are content to remain in diapers long after their parents have decided it's time for a change. If you have waited until now to toilet-train in the hope that your child will initiate the process but have yet to see any interest on her part, there is no harm in nudging her along in positive ways. You might start by helping her identify the issue ("Look—Chloe and Anna use the potty now") and formulate a goal ("Do you want to learn to use a potty, too?"). If she still fails to respond, point out occasionally that someone she admires uses a toilet instead of a diaper, show her the big-kid underwear at a store and ask her if she'd like some for herself, or remove her diaper while she's playing, set a potty nearby, and let her make a game out of using it. These attempts may not "take" the first, second, or third time you try them, but eventually your child will get the idea. (At no time should you try teasing or criticizing her for not responding to your suggestions. Such negative approaches not only backfire in practical terms but can hurt your child's self-esteem as well.)

Keep in mind that a reluctant child may simply be waiting for more direction—for you to take the next step by helping her create and carry out a plan.

the signals her body gives her and to use them as spurs to action: "Joanne, you're squirming around a lot. Does your tummy feel funny? That means you need to pee."

Remind her of what needs to be done to succeed at this skill: "I know it's hard to stop playing when you're having so much fun, but when you need to use the potty, it's important to go right away. Come on, I'll help you." Support her in unfamiliar situations: "If you need to use the potty at Julie's house, tell her mommy and she'll show you where it is."

Point out how much better she feels after she's used the potty and how nice it is to know she won't wet her pants this time. Like a coach encouraging a player to perform well, your goal is not to totally control her learning process; rather, some direction with ongoing reminders and helpful suggestions will facilitate the toilet-training process.

One of the strongest motivating forces for a preschooler mastering a new skill is his parents' praise. When your child succeeds at any of the steps involved in toilet training— picturing a goal ("I wanna wear underwear like Daddy!"), creating a plan ("If I have to go, I'll call you"), or actually achieving his goal ("Daddy, look, I did it!")—be sure to reinforce his feelings of satisfaction with a hug and a kiss. Restate his achievement ("Look at that, Ronnie, you pooped in the potty!") and let him know he should feel good about it ("You must feel proud"). Finally, express your own satisfaction clearly by letting him hear you report his success to others in the family ("Guess what Ronnie did today? He pooped in the potty—just like Sam") and even offering him a small reward such as a gold star on his potty chart. When accidents occur, let him accept responsibility for this experience as well by asking him to help you clean up (if he resists, calmly insist that he comply). Such natural consequences of his own actions motivate him to try harder and in the long run are much more effective than criticism or anger.

### There's Power in Numbers: The Benefits of Peer Pressure

"I went to the bathroom with Eric today," four-year-old Frank reports to his parents over dinner.

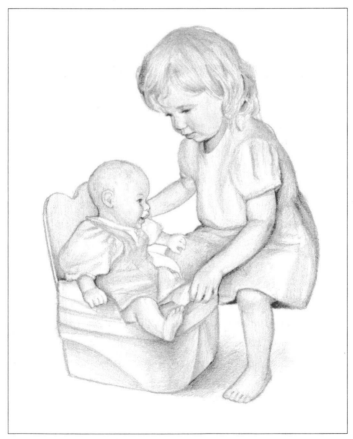

Teaching a doll to use the potty may help your imaginative child's progress during toilet training.

"That's nice, Frank," his dad says with a glance at his wife. "Did you use the potty all by yourself?"

"I peed in the toilet!" Frank says proudly, helping himself to more bread. "Eric peed, too. We made an X with our pee!"

Frank's parents exchange a smile as Frank laughs with delight over his exploit. They know that the joy Frank takes in sharing his toilet-training skills with a friend is a powerful motivator. Preschoolers' expanding social awareness—their love of observing and categorizing all aspects of their peers' behavior, from what they eat for lunch to whether they wear diapers or underpants—feeds a growing desire to be like

## PERSONALITY HELPS: LEVERAGING LEARNING STYLE TO MAKE TOILET TRAINING MORE EFFICIENT

In Chapter 4 you learned how much easier toilet training can be when you adapt your approach to suit your child's natural temperament, whether she is physically active or highly verbal, shy or gregarious. As your preschooler's personality grows steadily clearer, you may wish to further tailor your approach to fit with her emerging tastes. If you have learned, for example, that your child responds best to a predictable routine, it makes sense to focus on fitting regular "potty sessions" into her day and not worry as much about verbally reviewing her progress.

If she spends a lot of her time in imaginary play, tailor your approach to toilet training using imagi-

their friends. While this aspect of a child's development can work against his toilet-training progress at age two and a half or three, when he may decide he wants to revert to diapers because so many children at the childcare center wear them, it becomes a more positive force as toilet use becomes more common among his classmates.

You can take advantage of this natural tendency to conform by pointing out, in a nonjudgmental way, which of the children your own child knows who have also learned to use the potty. Keep in mind the fact that preschoolers are more likely to imitate people they most like or admire.

nary play. Help her show her doll how to properly use the potty. Talk to her stuffed animals and dolls and praise them for successfully going potty. Repeating these important steps using stuffed animals or dolls will help your child learn the steps of toilet training better than if you just gave her straightforward instructions and expected her to be able to follow them.

Taking the time to think about how your child learns best can help you as a parent facilitate the best training process—for her. By adapting your program to what you know works best for your child, and discarding the techniques that you've seen have little effect, you may succeed in limiting the critical part of toilet training to one or two weeks—and encounter less resistance in the process. This can be a real benefit to parents concerned about preschool or other toilet training deadlines.

So this is a time to keep an open mind about the many aspects of toilet use that captivate young children. While we may not quite understand the thrill of sharing a bathroom stall with a friend, communal voiding has helped many a preschooler succeed at and enjoy toilet training.

## A PARENT'S STORY

### "We All Made Poop!"

"My daughter, Beatrice, loved her first year of preschool, but at first I wondered if all she was going to learn there was how to go to the bathroom. Every day when I picked her up I'd ask her what she'd done that day, and invariably her reports were about the group trip to the bathroom. She was obviously fascinated by the whole business of standing in line, going into the bathroom stalls one by one, hearing the potty flush, seeing a child emerge successful, and so on. Later that night she'd tell her dad and her brother that she and the other kids 'all made poop today.' After it passed—and it did pass, after a month or so—I realized that it was just a natural part of processing the fact that others use the potty just as she does. In a funny way, it made her feel a real member of the group."

Judy, mother of Beatrice

Your preschooler is certainly thrilled to learn the ways he is like and unlike the children he knows, but this is a time

when a strong urge to conform with same-gender adult behavior manifests itself as well. Fascinated as they often are by
the concept of gender, three- and four-year-olds still have a
limited understanding of what constitutes the different genders. They are easily confused—assuming, for example, that
a teenage boy with a ponytail is a girl or that a girl with short
hair and a baseball cap is a boy.

Bathroom use is one obvious way to discern differences
between genders and to solidify one's own sense of gender. As
a result, a male preschooler may take great pride in urinating
standing up "just like Daddy," and a girl this age may enjoy
using the potty while Mommy puts on her makeup nearby.
Again, it's best to use this natural tendency to categorize in
your child's favor. Wanting to use the bathroom "like a boy"
or "like a girl" is a signal that your child is exploring all aspects of what it means to be him- or herself.

## "Let's Talk About It": Overcoming Obstacles

Toilet-training an older child is not just about productive
conversation, determined self-mastery, and an eager desire to
conform to big-kid behavior. Preschoolers' progress can be
delayed, and their parents' frustration increased, by such typical behaviors as contrariness (frequently resisting direction,
often by doing the opposite of what she is told) and increased
negotiation—as well as the new fears and anxieties that often
accompany their stage of development.

Contrariness springs from the same urge toward independence as the toddler's frequent "No!" As your child develops and her thinking grows more sophisticated, she
naturally longs to control more of her environment and direct a greater portion of her life. Just as she experimented

with defiant behaviors a year or two ago, your preschooler may now want to find out what will happen if she "forgets" to use the potty as you reminded her to do or if she decides she wants to wear diapers again after you have agreed that it's time to move on.

Such resistance is perfectly normal, but it can easily derail the toilet-training process. One way to discourage resistance is to withdraw from the conflict—to make toilet training more your child's project and less your own. You can do this by easing the pressure somewhat—talking less about how it's going, letting her choose when to wear underwear, letting her add stickers to her own achievement chart instead of providing all the praise yourself. At first your child may take a few steps backward in her progress (she may wear nothing below the waist at home rather than put on the underwear she dislikes), but the natural consequences of her actions—her siblings' teasing (which should be stopped immediately), not being allowed to go outside—will soon cause her to stop. You can use your position of authority to allow some freedom in your child's learning to use the toilet, but training, by nature, does involve some direction with encouragement.

Highly verbal preschoolers may prefer making excuses, arguing, or negotiating to simply resisting through their actions. Your child may explain away constant accidents with "I forgot," refuse to visit the bathroom, or constantly bargain for bigger and better rewards when she succeeds. Again, the first step in overcoming this kind of resistance is to stop engaging. Your verbal child loves nothing more than an interesting discussion or argument; if you refuse to participate, she will soon lose interest in this game. Avoid arguments and negotiation by keeping the rules simple (no

# "LOOK WHAT LILY DID!": DEALING WITH SHAME

Not all aspects of preschoolers' expanding social awareness support their toilet-training progress in healthy ways. Their fascination with different behaviors and categories of people can lead to exclusion, negative comments, teasing, and other negative responses toward children who are still in diapers. Such shaming behavior is obviously painful to a three- or four-year-old and should not be discounted or ignored if it happens to your child. Certainly you will want to counter the negative remarks with supportive comments of your own, and talk with the adults in charge about stopping such behavior in the future.

Yet negative experiences of this kind are often inevitable and can be used in positive ways—as a kind of springboard to toilet-training success. After comforting and reassuring your child, consider talking with her about whether she's ready to take the next step in growing up. Offer to let her practice wearing underwear around the house for a few days to see whether she wants to start trying to use the toilet. Show her how you'll support her with reminders, routine bathroom visits, and other reassuring techniques. Let her know that all children make a few mistakes as they move from diapers to underwear, but that sooner or later everyone achieves success.

bedtime story if there's no visit to the bathroom first; one gold star and a big hug for each successful session on the potty) and never making an exception because that can extend the behavior even more. Meanwhile, you can use your child's love of words to your advantage by talking to her about how the body works, remarking on her progress, and elaborating on how free and independent she'll feel once she's out of diapers.

Fears and anxiety regarding toilet use are other problems that can surface during the preschool years as children's imaginations expand. A child who has no trouble sitting on her potty may experience terror on an adult-size toilet as she

Establishing a daily bathroom routine and keeping your child company can lessen her fears and anxiety surrounding potty use.

imagines monsters crawling out to grab her or fears that she will be flushed away. Even potties create anxiety for some children, who worry about sitting over an empty bowl or releasing their stool (part of their body) into it.

If your child resists going to the bathroom or seems fearful or anxious during potty or toilet use, try keeping her company while she voids. While doing this, you can help by flushing the toilet for her, encouraging her to flush bits of toilet paper, letting her accompany you and other family members to the bathroom, and otherwise reassuring her in concrete ways that there is nothing to be afraid of.

Preschoolers' increased verbal skills make it easier to talk gently about what might be upsetting them—but because three- and four-year-olds still have limited vocabularies and comprehension, you may need to listen and carefully observe to uncover the nature of the problem. Once you have done so, don't downplay its importance to your child. Saying "That's silly" or "There's no witch in the bathroom" will only make her think you don't understand. Instead, take the time to work through her fear or anxiety with her—explaining how a monster couldn't possibly fit inside the toilet, putting a favorite doll on the potty and pretending to let it poop, and otherwise using words to increase her level of confidence.

Fortunately, your child's natural urge to develop and grow will carry her through most of the difficult stages of toilet training without a huge amount of effort on your part. During the preschool years, when peer pressure and big-kid ambitions play such a major role, toilet training becomes less an issue of directing your child and more one of staying out of the way enough to let her direct herself. By refusing to magnify problems, you will find that most soon vanish and your child is on the road to bathroom success again.

## Q & A

### "What Will Her Friends Think?"

**Q:** My four-year-old daughter is in her second year of preschool and still has accidents occasionally. Recently she's been invited along on day trips by a couple of her classmates. I hesitate to let her go because her accidents usually happen when she's in an unfamiliar place. How can she participate in these activities without being embarrassed?

**A:** Time is your ally in such situations: the older your child is and the more practice she has had controlling her bladder even in unfamiliar settings, the less likely she will be to have accidents when off with her friends. You can help her avoid such incidents by talking with her about the need to monitor her body's signals, to tell an adult that she needs to go, and to adjust to different kinds of bathrooms. Applaud all of her efforts to be self-sufficient (finding a bathroom herself, dealing with her own clothes), since increased confidence will help her avoid future accidents. And don't let your own concerns about her embarrassment keep you from letting her share fun times with friends. When you do send her off for the day, pack a small bag with extra clothes and wipes for the friend's parent to take along. Most parents will understand your concern and handle such a situation tactfully.

Q:    I am a single mother and lately have had some problems accompanying my four-year-old son to the bathroom in public places. He doesn't want to go into the women's room with me, and I can't go to the men's room with him. But he still needs help with his clothes sometimes, and I don't want to leave him in a public place alone. What should I do?

A:    Helping an opposite-sex child on the toilet is certainly easier during the toddler years. Fortunately, many public areas such as airports not only have gender-specific bathrooms but also have family bathrooms that you and your child can use. As children grow and become more aware of gender differences—and more aware of their surroundings in general—public bathrooms can become an uncomfortable place for both parent and child. It is best to take your child to the bathroom corresponding with your own gender through at least age four. After that, if he objects or if you feel uncomfortable, you may decide to send him into his own gender's bathroom while you wait within hearing distance right outside the door. First, though, help him practice removing and refastening his clothes, flushing the toilet and washing his hands, and performing all the other routines of bathroom use that you have been reinforcing up to now. Now is also a good time to reinforce the concept of "private parts" and to instruct him to come to you immediately if he is approached in the bathroom by someone he doesn't know.

**Q:** My three-year-old daughter's interest in toilet training has come with an unfortunate side effect: potty talk. While I am happy to see her learning to use her potty with relative ease, I am very tired of hearing the words *poopy-head, butt,* and *pee-pee* shouted out in public places, followed by gales of laughter. How can I stop this kind of talk without dampening my child's interest in her potty?

**A:** Bathroom humor, or potty talk, commonly accompanies toilet training and preschool development in general. Three- and four-year-olds become interested in these words as they hear them increasingly from you during toilet training or from their friends during play. Not only do these new terms seem to hold the key to the puzzle of how their bodies work and why boys and girls differ—two issues that fascinate children at this age—but they offer the added punch of terrific shock value. Saying "poopy-head" is bound to get a strong reaction from you and plenty of laughter from your daughter's friends. What preschooler could resist such a word?

You can discourage this behavior by taking care not to overreact to it. If your child gets no shocked response, using the words is not as much fun. Calmly acknowledge her motive for using such terms ("That word sounds funny to you, huh?"), then redirect her attention ("I know a good joke. Listen to this..."). It is not too soon, also, to start teaching your child that certain behavior is appropriate in some situations but not in others ("Talk about bathroom stuff with Mom and Dad, not with your brother's friends"). As long as you don't expect perfect results right away and don't focus too intensely on this issue, it will pass.

## CHAPTER 6

# BEYOND TOILET TRAINING: COMMON PROBLEMS AND THEIR CAUSES

Stacy and Hal's daughter, Lindy, was toilet-trained at the early age of twenty-four months with surprisingly few of the problems her playmates eventually faced. For more than a year she was using a potty. Of course, there were some accidents, particularly during the first six months following toilet training, but fewer accidents overall than her parents had expected.

Now that Lindy was four and attending preschool, however, a new challenge presented itself. Lindy had started leaking small amounts of urine once or twice a day. Her parents frequently found that her underwear was slightly damp when Lindy got home from school or when she undressed for her bath at night. It wasn't that she was having accidents—she still easily stopped what she was doing and went to the bathroom when she needed to urinate—but she seemed to experience a certain amount of dribbling between potty sessions that she was unable to control. The dampness didn't bother

Lindy, but her parents worried that a physical, developmental, or even emotional problem might be the cause.

As Lindy's situation indicates, issues relating to bladder and bowel control can arise not only during the actual toilet-training process but also long after parents assume that their children are fully trained. In many cases, such setbacks can be remedied with relative ease once the causes have been identified. Medical or psychological intervention may be necessary. No matter what the reason behind your own child's problem, the earlier you address the issue, the better the chances that it will be resolved without seriously affecting your child.

## FROM THE EXPERTS

### Setbacks Happen

"As a parent, you may be disappointed to discover that daytime toilet training, once accomplished, doesn't always last. Many children who have been well trained begin to experience frequent accidents later. Complete relapses in toilet training can also occur.

"There are a number of reasons for this. In some cases, children manage to stay dry during the initial toilet-training process by fully focusing on this issue—but as they become more involved in other activities, the number of accidents increases. Changes in a child's life, changes in family dynamics, or a new stage of development can also lead to changes in bathroom behavior. Since nighttime wetting is more a function of physiological development than a training issue, it can easily continue for months or even years after daytime dryness has been achieved, to age six and beyond in some cases. Frequently the pattern of nighttime wetting runs in families, so if this condition has occurred in other family members, it is more likely to happen in your child.

"The point is, toilet-training setbacks happen to most children in one form or another, though such issues are rarely discussed outside the family. Toilet-training is an ongoing learning process for your child, not a cut-and-dried program that is completed in a couple of weeks. You will probably find that your child's problem is not unusual. The sooner you can ascertain its cause and provide the appropriate support, the better for your child."

Barbara J. Howard, MD, FAAP

This chapter identifies many of the most common problems experienced by young children who have completed toilet training, lists the most common reasons behind such behaviors, and offers general guidelines for parents to follow in correcting them. Still, there is no substitute for the individual advice of your child's pediatrician. A conversation with, or a visit to, your child's doctor is the first step in combating any disturbing or ongoing issue.

## "I Just Can't!": Physical Challenges

Many negative behaviors related to young children's toilet use result from physical problems that can be easily identified and resolved by your pediatrician. Certainly, physical causes are the first possibility to investigate when your child seems stuck in a negative behavior and unable to find a way out.

Such was the case with Lindy in the situation described above. Her pediatrician concluded after talking briefly with Lindy and her parents, and giving Lindy a brief physical examination, that the minor leaks she experienced were due to Lindy waiting too long before going to the bathroom. Based on recommendations from the doctor, her parents had her void every two hours, and they also had her drink more water to fill her bladder so that she would better recognize the need to go to the bathroom. They also showed her how to position herself on the toilet so that her feet were supported. They taught her how to take deep breaths in and out to help her relax her pelvic muscles so that she could completely empty her bladder.

Your own child may experience frequent dampness or leaks for quite different reasons—say, a small bladder capacity that requires her to go to the bathroom more frequently than she's willing to; a "lazy bladder" that leads to peeing only once or twice a day, with overflows at other times; lack of coordination between the bladder muscle and the sphincter (the ringlike muscle involved in controlling bowel movements); insufficient exercise, leading to poor muscle control; or even emotional stress, which can create irritation of the bladder walls.

Some of these situations, such as small bladder capacity, will probably soon be outgrown. Others, such as poor muscle coordination, can be remedied through biofeedback and, possibly, prescribed medications. Some may require changes in other aspects of your life, such as instituting a regular schedule of bathroom visits or reducing the stress that is affecting your child's functioning.

Your pediatrician is the best resource to prescribe the right combination of medication, behavior modification, or other treatment for your child. If need be, the doctor can also refer you to a pediatric urologist. He can also identify or rule out serious conditions such as diabetes, urinary tract infections, or neurological problems (as indicated by increased frequency of urination). Finally, he can help identify nonphysical causes of incontinence, including poor bathroom habits—for example, a girl may be urinating while holding her legs together, thus retaining urine that leaks out later. Other nonphysical causes may involve such normal aspects of child development as testing parental boundaries, overfocusing on other activities and ignoring the body's signals, or having difficulty verbalizing fears, anxieties, and physical discomfort relating to bathroom use.

### Constipation

Surprisingly, constipation is another common cause of daytime and nighttime wetting. Infrequent bowel movements or hard stools can push against your child's bladder, decreasing its capacity to hold urine. Constipation can also lead to urinary tract infections, which can in turn negatively affect urination. Studies have shown that in a large majority of cases in which children suffer from both urinary incontinence and chronic constipation, eliminating constipation helps solve the wetting problems, too.

Constipation is when your child has developed large and hard stool, making it difficult and possibly painful to have a bowel movement. This is almost certainly the case if she resists having a bowel movement, complains that it hurts to poop, strains a great deal when having a bowel movement, and urinates more than usual, yet produces a dry, hard stool.

Her discomfort should be addressed right away, since painful elimination can negatively alter a young child's bathroom habits and grow more painful and intractable quite quickly.

Contact your child's pediatrician as soon as you notice signs of constipation, and start taking notes on when she urinates or moves her bowels, how much is voided, and how much and under what circumstances she wets. (See the box on page 124.) Meanwhile, avoid insisting that your child stay on the toilet and "keep trying." Sitting and pushing for long periods can cause hemorrhoids or small tears (called anal fissures) in the wall of the anus. Instead, have her try more frequently—particularly after meals and before bedtime—for no more than five minutes at a time, with the goal of having a bowel movement nearly every day.

Make sure that your child drinks plenty of water. Instead of having her sip all day, have her drink three glasses of water (with each glass equal in volume to the child's age + 2 in ounces) in ten minutes. For example, a four-year-old would drink three 6-ounce glasses of water in ten minutes). Eating foods high in fiber, such as whole-wheat bread, brown rice, fresh fruits, and vegetables, will help soften your child's stools. Avoid high-fat or greasy foods, peanut butter, chocolate, dairy products, and sweets. Also, see to it that your child gets enough exercise to move waste through her body. Explaining that such changes will help her feel more comfortable—and remaining firm in your decision—will help her adjust to her new regimen.

If constipation continues and your child complains of increased pain, chances are that the passage of hard, dry stools has created an anal fissure or other irritation. Soothe the irritation by applying a small amount of petroleum jelly on your child's bottom before a bowel movement, if possible, and immediately afterward. Soon, as her stools begin to soften and the irritated area is protected, the pain will go away and bowel movements will become easier to complete.

## "HOW CAN I TELL?"

### Symptoms of Urinary Tract Infection

A number of common symptoms indicate the possibility of a urinary tract infection (UTI). Look for the following symptoms in your child:

- Fever
- Pain or burning during urination
- Urgent need to urinate, or wetting of underwear or bedding by a toilet-trained child
- Vomiting, refusal to eat
- Abdominal pain
- Side or back pain
- Foul-smelling urine
- Cloudy or bloody urine

If your child has symptoms of a UTI, your pediatrician will do the following:

- Ask about your child's symptoms
- Ask about any family history of urinary tract problems
- Ask what medications your child is taking, if any

## Fecal Soiling

Fecal soiling, referred to medically as *encopresis* in children over four years of age, affects about 1.5 percent of young schoolchildren, with boys outnumbering girls by a ratio of six to one. While much less common than accidental

- Examine your child
- Get a urine sample from your child

Your pediatrician will need to test your child's urine to see if there are bacteria or other abnormalities. If your child is old enough (usually above age three), she will probably be asked to provide a urine sample by urinating into a container. If this is not possible and/or your pediatrician needs a sterile specimen to make a definitive judgment about an infection, he may need to place a small tube, called a catheter, through the urethra into the bladder. Urine flows through the tube into a special urine container.

Keep in mind that UTIs are common and most are easy to treat. Such infections are especially common among preschool-age girls. Early diagnosis and prompt treatment are important because untreated or repeated infections can cause long-term medical problems. Talk to your pediatrician if you suspect that your child might have a UTI. Your pediatrician will probably prescribe an antibiotic if an infection is present.

# WHAT YOUR PEDIATRICIAN NEEDS TO KNOW

## Keeping a Bathroom Journal

Daytime wetting and constipation can occur for a wide variety of physiological and psychological reasons. During your child's examination, your pediatrician will need to consider a large number of possible causes. You can make this process much more productive and efficient by keeping a bathroom journal for at least a day, and preferably several days, before the appointment. If your child attends a childcare center or preschool, have the caregivers keep a record of her bathroom habits when she is there, and you can continue to track her habits when you both get home. If that is not an option, keep the diary over the weekend when you are home with your child.

Here are some points to keep in mind:

- Begin your diary by listing a few facts about your child's toilet training. Write down the age at which she was toilet-trained and describe any physical or behavioral difficulties she had at that time.
- List any infections, pain, or puzzling behaviors she has exhibited since that time, as well as any medication she has taken or is taking. Any of these may affect her bathroom habits.
- If she is having trouble at daycare, preschool, or elsewhere, make a note of this, too.
- Once you have filled in this background information, begin noting when your child urinates

and defecates, approximately how much urine or stool is released at each session, and the size, color, and consistency of the stool.

- Describe any related behavior before, during, and after potty use—such as anxiously clutching her genitals, peeing before she gets to the potty, being unable to urinate once she's in the bathroom, passing loose stools but appearing constipated, racing away before the toilet can be flushed, and so on.

Note also when accidents occur, approximately how much urine is released at these times, and whether any specific behavior is associated with these events. Some warning signs are especially important to point out to your pediatrician. These include any significant amount of blood in the urine or stool, unusually large volumes of urine, urine that is unusually diluted (lighter in color than normal), weakness or pain in the back or legs, or an increase in the frequency of wetting or constipation.

Keeping a written record of your child's behavior over several days can prove much more helpful than casual observation, since it can be easy to overlook important signals in the rush of everyday life. By acting as your pediatrician's "field scout" and gathering important information ahead of time, you can speed up the process of cure and recovery enormously—saving your child unnecessary confusion and pain.

(Adapted from "Daytime Wetting: Getting to the Bottom of the Issue" by Anthony J. Casale, MD, *Contemporary Pediatrics*, vol. 17, no. 2 [2000].)

urination or minor leaks, it can be more upsetting to both parent and child. Not only is the odor more noticeable and disturbing, but children as young as two are expected in our culture to "know better" than to soil their pants. In most cases, however, fecal soiling is not voluntary but occurs when emotional stress, resistance to toilet training, or physical pain during bowel movements causes a child to resist having bowel movements. This resistance, or stool retention, leads to constipation, which in turn leads to involuntary leakage or soiling when the pressure becomes too great.

If this continues to happen, the muscles involved in stool ejection may begin to stretch and nerve sensations in the area

## MANAGING CONSTIPATION

Frequent constipation that does not respond to changes in your child's diet and physical activity requires a pediatrician's attention. Your child may be reacting to dairy products or other foods. In rare instances, chronic constipation may be caused by gastrointestinal disease or by anatomical or neurological disorders.

While you are waiting to meet with your pediatrician, refrain from giving your child laxatives, enemas, or stool softeners to ease her discomfort. The American Academy of Pediatrics does not recommend the use of such over-the-counter remedies except on the advice of a pediatrician. Focus on treating the cause of your child's problem, not the symptoms.

## "DOESN'T IT BOTHER HER?"

Many parents are shocked to smell the results of fecal soiling. Naturally, they expect their child to be equally surprised and embarrassed by the situation—yet this is not always the case. Your child may simply be too young to understand how unusual and unwelcome such a smell is. If soiling has occurred frequently for her, she may have become accustomed to the smell and actually fails to notice it anymore. Some children may even act as if soiling is no big deal because they realize they can't control it.

If you find that your child doesn't seem to care that her clothes have been soiled, a talk about cleanliness certainly has its place. Rather than making her feel ashamed, however, focus on having her help you clean her up and then change her clothes, encourage her to go to the toilet next time, and look for any underlying causes such as constipation.

diminish, making it more difficult for the child to feel the need to defecate. The intestines may lose their ability to contract, making bowel movements even more of a challenge and fecal soiling more likely.

In most cases, the best way to approach the problem of fecal soiling due to constipation is to address the underlying issue that is causing your child to resist having a bowel movement. He may stop retaining stool if you ease the pressure to use the potty, for example, or if you stay with him while he poops—and as his bowel movements become more regular, his fecal soiling may disappear.

If the problem continues beyond one or two accidents, however, be sure to make an appointment with your child's pediatrician, who will review your child's medical history to determine whether a physical condition rather than stool retention may be causing the soiling. Congenital megacolon or Hirschsprung's disease (a congenital condition that prevents a child from feeling the sensation of having a full bowel), ulcerative colitis, allergies, or even a diet containing too many dairy products or high-fat foods can sometimes lead to accidental soiling.

If these physical causes have also been eliminated, emotional or psychological causes should be considered. Fecal soiling can occur when a child is anxious or emotionally distraught over some aspect of his life over which he has little control, such as family conflicts, academic difficulties, or problems with social relationships. Physical and sexual abuse may also need to be considered if soiling continues.

Of course, it is quite possible for any young child to have even this kind of accident once or twice. No matter what the cause, your child needs to understand that what has happened is not his fault. As with bedwetting, the situation is best corrected by quickly cleaning up, avoiding shame and embarrassment as much as possible, and providing him with the information he needs to better control his bowel movements and keep his clothes clean. Once your child's feelings are protected, you can take action to identify the underlying cause, with the understanding that a remedy may take some time.

## Medical Examinations

As important as it is to have your child examined by a pediatrician when you suspect a physical cause for her accidents, soiling, or constipation, keep in mind how uncomfortable some examinations may be for her. In addressing practically any type of wetting or constipation issue, your child's pediatrician will probably knead or palpate your child's abdomen; observe her lower back, buttocks, external genitalia, and anus; examine her characteristic walk; and observe her ability to climb onto the examination table.

The pediatrician may ask your child to urinate into a cup so that her urine can be tested and analyzed. If she is unable to do this, a sample may be obtained by passing a catheter through the urethra into the bladder. Your child may also be given a rectal exam. The pediatrician will ask a number of questions about how long the problem has existed, when and where it occurs, whether and where there is pain, and so on.

Some aspects of this initial examination—and any meetings with specialists that may follow—may include procedures such as ultrasound, magnetic resonance imaging (MRI), or VCUG (a voiding cystourethrogram, in which a dye is placed in the bladder via a catheter and then monitored by X-rays). These tests may be upsetting to your child. You know best whether a physical exam, testing with bulky equipment, or probing questions are likely to frighten her.

Before meeting with the doctor, take the time to talk with your child about the examination, preparing her for what she may consider the more scary procedures without frightening her or going into too much detail. Young children often respond better to role playing, through puppets and toys, casual conversation, and physical reassurance than to direct instruction and explanation.

Once at the pediatrician's or specialist's office, assure your child that you will stay by her side unless she wants you to leave (if you are sure this will be possible). Ask her whether there's anything she wants to tell the doctor before he begins the exam. Respect her need to take things slowly and control as much of the process as possible, and avoid tests that your pediatrician believes are unnecessary.

## "I Don't Understand!": Social and Environmental Obstacles

If your child's pediatrician has ruled out physical causes for your child's problems with toilet use, it is time to consider possible environmental factors. Your child's daily interactions with you and other adults, as well as with her siblings and peers, can have a decided effect on her bathroom behavior.

Issues centering around childcare can create complications as well—particularly when both parents work full-time and the child is cared for by other adults for long periods of time. Sometimes the difficulty is caused by conflicting attitudes among the adults involved in monitoring bathroom behavior. Perhaps you have no problem with the fact that your four-year-old is not yet toilet-trained, while his babysitter resents having to change diapers. Or you may be battling a recent rash of accidents by keeping your child on a regular bathroom schedule at home, only to find that she has wet her pants at school because she wasn't sent to the bathroom after lunch.

Finding a solution to such problems requires discussing

what is happening with all the adults involved in your child's care. Describe any problems and the plans you have created to solve them. Solicit the other adults' opinions about these plans, and listen to their objections or suggestions.

Then come to an agreement about a course of action, so that your child will meet with a consistent response everywhere she goes. Ideally, because you are the parent, your decision should be the final one, but there may be times when it's more practical or productive to follow another caregiver's lead. If the childcare center schedules five bathroom visits a day, for example, you can schedule visits to the home bathroom at the same times.

It's important to discuss resistant behavior and other training problems with all the adults involved in your child's care, so that plans can be made to remedy the situation and avoid accidents.

Be sure to follow up such discussions by asking for feedback about how the techniques used seem to be affecting your child. If she is increasingly resisting a rigid bathroom schedule, it may be better to allow her to choose when she goes—even at her childcare center or preschool. If her accidents seem to occur when she is engrossed in story hour, perhaps she can be taken to the bathroom before the story begins.

No matter how embarrassing you believe your child's problem is, it is necessary to seek out this kind of support. Rest assured that caregivers are accustomed to dealing with everything from fecal soiling to genital exploration to frequent experiments with potty talk. There is little your child can do that will shock or even surprise a professional caregiver or educator. By asking for their support and advice, you may receive some welcome support for your own efforts as well.

## Adjusting to Multiple Households

For children who move between two separate homes, usually as a result of parents' separation or divorce, problems can arise from inconsistent or conflicting approaches to bathroom use. In situations like this, it is vital that parents communicate with each other about the rules and routines that they intend to maintain. Such negotiations can be difficult, of course, since both parents have equal authority and may have sharply divergent opinions. Still, it is important for your child's sake to keep the bathroom routine as consistent as possible between the two homes—using the same type of potty when possible, for example, and keeping it in the same room in each home—and to respond to new challenges as a team.

## Travel

A change in environment caused by a vacation or other travel is another common cause of bathroom-related problems among young children. Travel plans that call for a break in a child's routine, or that take the child away from a familiar bathroom or potty, may create anxiety that then leads to accidents or constipation. While most such responses are only temporary and disappear once the child is used to the new routine or has returned to the old one, some lead to negative learned behavior, such as withholding stool or delaying urination, that takes weeks or months to correct.

## A PARENT'S STORY

### Different Places, Different Rules

"My husband and I went through a difficult divorce when our son, Max, was one. By the time Max was toilet-trained at age three, Colin and I lived in separate houses at opposite ends of town. Max alternated between us, living one week with Colin and the next with me, and his dad set up details of domestic life in completely different ways than I did. I made dinner for Max every evening at five o'clock. With his dad, he ate dinner out most nights at around eight. I let Max wear training pants at night. His dad insisted he wear underwear. I kept Max's potty in the bathroom. His dad kept it in Max's bedroom.

"I tried to talk this issue over with Colin, but he refused to change any of his routines. I tried to change mine to accommodate Colin's, but some of the changes just didn't work for me. Meanwhile, Max had started to have accidents again. He even started pooping in his bedroom—since that was where he used the potty at his dad's house.

"Finally I decided to sit Max down and talk to him about 'different places, different rules.' By then he was nearly four, old enough to understand that people do things in different ways and that one way isn't necessarily better or worse—just different. Once I brought up the subject, he seemed very eager to talk about all the funny differences between his two homes. After that talk, I was able to just say, 'Remember, Max, different rules!' at bedtime, and chances were he would remember that in my house the potty was in the bathroom.

"I guess the moral of this story would be that cooperation between parents is always best. But if you can't cooperate fully, it isn't the end of the world. Kids can handle differences in routine more and more as they get older."

Kelly, mother of Max

To avoid such complications, it's best to keep your child's bathroom experience while traveling as similar as possible to the routine he follows at home. If you are traveling by car, consider taking your child's potty along. When flying, take your child to the bathroom at the airport before you board the plane, and bring along familiar stuffed animals or other favorite objects that may make public or hotel bathrooms less frightening. Plan to accompany your child to the bathroom and expect to prompt him toward bathroom use more than if you were not traveling.

### "It Was an Accident!": Emotional Issues

Emotional causes of bathroom-related problems are among the most challenging to address, since young children are rarely able to express their confusion, anxiety, or fear in words. Such behaviors as defecating in a corner of the bedroom, having daily accidents at school after many months of complete dryness, or pleading to return to diapers are disturbing and even frightening to many parents—more so when they do not understand the cause. Once physical causes have been ruled out, however, the reasons behind many of these behaviors can be unearthed by considering any changes in your child's life or emotional development, observing her other behaviors, and listening carefully to what she says.

---

PARENT POTTY TIPS

Young children who are still unsure of their bathroom skills may feel especially threatened by a change in their environment or routine—whether they are starting preschool or visiting Grandma's house. Experienced parents offer the following suggestions to help children manage such changes while maintaining good bathroom habits. Consider these before your next vacation or other major change.

**Offer him training pants.** Though your toilet-trained child may balk at the idea of returning to training pants—he doesn't want to "be a baby"—he may accept the idea of wearing them under his underwear until he's sure he can handle the change. This hidden support will help him maintain confidence and prevent embarrassment.

**Don't give him water** or any other beverage right before you leave the house or begin your trip. He will appreciate every extra minute he gets before he needs to use the bathroom in a strange new place.

**Have him use the bathroom at home before you leave.** Again, this will give him more time to adjust to his new surroundings.

**Bring a full change of clothes.** No matter how you try to prevent them, accidents can still happen. Avoid extra discomfort by changing your child into dry clothes immediately.

**Talk before you go.** Make a point of explaining to your child where he will be going, whom he will be visiting, and how he will use the bathroom while he's on his journey. Walk through several possible scenarios with him. Role-play with puppets or stuffed animals if he enjoys that. Assure him that you will accompany him to the bathroom if he wants you to. On your first bathroom visit with him away from home, point out the features you described when you were at home. Let him observe you using the bathroom first, if he wants to, and stand by as he tries, as you said you would.

If you discover your child trying to hide her accidents, provide her with gentle reassurance and discuss ways the two of you can succeed in the future.

In Chapter 4 you learned how a major change in a child's life can cause her to regress during toilet training. Regression can occur for similar reasons long after toilet training has been accomplished. A new baby in the family, a move to a new house, family conflict, or any other emotionally stressful situation may cause your child to revert to an earlier level of bathroom mastery—possibly involving bedwetting, withholding of stool, or even defecating in inappropriate places. Inner stress prompted by your child's normal development can affect her bathroom behaviors, too.

At about three years of age, children begin to develop the capacity to experience discomfort, or shame, when they have done something they know is wrong—yet most children this age do not know what to do with these feelings. A child who longs for her parents' approval may suddenly start to feel embarrassed or ashamed when a bathroom accident occurs, no matter how accepting her parents are actually likely to be. As a result, she may claim to have used the bathroom when she really urinated on the living room floor. She may hide her wet underwear, or even try to clean up the mess before you see it. There is certainly no cause to criticize or punish a child who behaves in this way. On the contrary, she has demonstrated that she knows what proper bathroom behavior is and is trying as best she can to make it "come true." The best response when you find your child hiding her accidents from you is to gently tell her that you know she had an accident, that it's okay, and that you know she will do better next time. Then ask her to help you clean up, and talk with her about specific ways in which the two of you can help her get back on track.

Other feelings and emotional situations can overwhelm your young child and cause her to behave in ways that are initially puzzling. A desire for more attention may cause her to stage an increasing number of accidents just to engage you in conversation or emotional interaction. If she feels you have been too controlling about bathroom use—constantly asking her if she needs to go instead of letting her direct her own behavior—she may resist going until it's too late and she has an accident instead.

A more active imagination and a tendency toward magical thinking may cause her to fear the toilet and start to avoid it. Even a desire to befriend another child by imitating him can lead to regressive bathroom practices if the other child has not been toilet-trained. Finally, a temporary wish to return to coddled babyhood, which nearly all young children experience at some time, may prompt your child to ask you if she can start wearing diapers again.

For toilet-trained children, as well as for those still being trained, regression in bathroom use usually does not last long if parents respond calmly and use it as an opportunity to support and communicate with their child. Refer to Chapter 4 for advice on helping your child identify the problem, sympathizing with her feelings, helping her find practical solutions, and clarifying your expectations regarding toilet use. Such evidence of your support and understanding will help her to relax and eventually move forward. Meanwhile, try to avoid major, concrete concessions such as returning to diapers, but offer to put her in training pants under panties for a while, place the potty in her room, accompany her to the preschool bathroom before the school day begins, or otherwise compromise until she feels more secure.

## A PARENT'S STORY

### Two New Babies?

"When my first child was three and fully toilet-trained, I had another baby. Within three months my older child had started having bowel movements in his pants every day. I tried ignoring it, making him clean up the mess himself, even giving him time-outs. Nothing worked. Eventually, after another month or so, he started using the potty again on his own. Looking back, I guess I should have looked at the cause of his behavior (the birth of his brother) more than the symptoms (dirtying his pants). Then I could have at least been a little more understanding while he solved this problem himself."

Sandra, mother of Travis and Sam

# "WILL I GET FLUSHED DOWN?"
## AND OTHER TOILET-RELATED FEARS

"There's a monster in the toilet!" "What if I fall in?" "I hate that loud flushing noise." There are nearly as many fears about toilet use as there are older toddlers and preschoolers using the toilet. Sooner or later you are likely to spot your three- or four-year-old racing out of the bathroom to escape the flushing noise, or repeatedly flushing small objects down the toilet, fascinated to watch them disappear. Keep in mind when this happens that such fears are a normal aspect of an expanding imagination.

Toddlers and preschoolers also naturally lean toward animism—the belief that inanimate objects are alive. As with other forms of anxiety, you can best respond to such fears by asking your child what frightens her and then demonstrating as best you can that her fears are groundless. You may decide to use the toilet yourself while your child watches, to demonstrate its safety; allow a doll to fall into the toilet and then flush to prove

## "I Forgot": Cognitive Challenges

Some problematic toilet behaviors have physical origins. Others are caused by anxiety or other overwhelming emo-

that something that big can't be flushed down; or shine a flashlight in and around the bowl to show your child that there are no monsters in sight. You may also want to make toilet use easier by offering to flush for her after she leaves the bathroom, staying with her until she's finished, or letting her return to potty use for a while.

It is important to understand that your child may not know, or be able to explain to you, what it is about the toilet that makes her afraid. She may even tell you she is afraid to use the toilet when in fact she just doesn't want to. In either case, there is probably no need to dwell on the issue. After you have done what you can to demonstrate that the toilet is harmless, reiterate your expectation that she will use the bathroom like a big girl. Look the other way if she tries unusual ways to comply, such as sitting backward on the toilet seat or racing out of the bathroom after she's flushed and pulling up her pants in the hallway. Her fears will soon fade as a result of her natural development and, as in other aspects of her life, she finds a way to manage them.

tions. Many behaviors, however, are quite typical expressions of a normal child's ongoing cognitive development. Earlier chapters noted that younger toddlers need to develop the ability to comprehend and respond to the body's signals before parents attempt toilet training. Further developments that manifest over time can support or sabotage bathroom habits—and, in some cases, do both. Forgetfulness and distractibility continue to challenge children, whose memory capacity is still limited—particularly when a lot is happening or things are changing in their lives. Difficulty breaking focus in time to get to the bathroom leads to accidents as well.

Cognitive growth in toddlers and preschoolers allows them to think more about and test the limits parents impose— leading to deliberate violations of bathroom routines. At the same time, while preschoolers' greatly expanded imagination helps them think and learn about toilet use through play, it can lead to resistance as children imagine disaster looming each time the toilet is flushed. Enhanced imagination is also responsible for such "magical-thinking" practices as depositing stool in strange places, avoiding certain bathrooms or insisting on using only one particular potty, refusing to flush the toilet or flushing a ritual number of times, and so on.

Strange as some of these behaviors can appear to adults, they are perfectly reasonable from a child's point of view. Again, there is no point in criticizing your child for behavior he cannot help. In some cases, particularly those involving confusion about toilet use, a series of brief, thoughtful conversations may ease the situation. At other times, as when bathroom practices are violated as a way of testing boundaries, it's important to restate your rules and stand firmly behind them. As in the other instances described in this chapter, your knowledge of your particular child remains your best tool in deciding how to respond. As long as your child knows that you support his efforts but that you expect him to return soon to correct bathroom behavior, the two of you will eventually reach your goal.

## "She Did What?": Seeing Beyond Your Own Agenda

Most parents want the best for their children, and may even view their successes and failures as extensions of themselves. Bathroom behavior in particular—with its associations with cleanliness, decency, and civilized behavior—often calls up intense emotions that we may not have realized we had. This is why so many parents feel bewildered by bathroom mistakes that are actually quite common among toddlers and preschoolers. It is hard to keep in mind that such behaviors seem quite normal to our children, and to remember that they frequently occur in other families, too.

When addressing your child's current problem, try to set aside your own agenda—your expectations regarding her progress, your emotional response to her actions, your embarrassment over how her behavior looks to others—and focus instead on your child's need for information, attention, and support. If you feel yourself getting frustrated, ask your partner, a friend, or your child's caregiver to take over until you regain some balance.

If your child's behavior has you perplexed or confused, don't hesitate to ask your pediatrician for advice or reassurance. Other parents, most of whom have experienced or know of similar situations, can also provide insight or offer you a fresh perspective. Parenting classes are another excellent source of information on specific bathroom-related challenges. Remember—both you and your child are eager for her to move forward in her development, but only you can provide the knowledge and support she may need to progress.

## FROM THE EXPERTS

### Nobody's Perfect

"In my job as a preschool teacher, I deal with bathroom-related issues every week, if not every day. I can certainly assure parents that many supposedly toilet-trained three- and four-year-olds have accidents now and then, particularly when they're in a new situation that requires more focused attention. These mishaps are part of the process of growing up, and nothing to worry about.

"I think it would help a lot if parents think about toilet training not as a one-time learning experience that's completed in a week or a month but as a skill that kids get better at as they mature. While they're practicing the skill, parents should try to be sensitive to their feelings. In most cases a child will get back on track after only one or two incidents, or maybe two weeks of regressing at the most."

Bibi Stevens, teacher

## Q & A

### Should We Worry?

**Q:**    Our three-year-old son has been toilet-trained for about four months, but he still has an accident every day or two. My wife says this is a normal part of the training process. It seems to me that a child his age should be doing better by now and that maybe he has a developmental problem. Which of us is right?

**A:**   Your wife is correct in saying that accidents sometimes continue for months after the toilet-training process appears to be complete—even when a child is three or four years old. Such daytime accidents are part of learning new physical habits and should start to taper off after about six months. (Nighttime wetting can continue much longer—see Chapter 8.)

You are also correct, however, when you point out that quite frequent accidents in a three-year-old—particularly when they do not seem to be diminishing—may signal a physical or developmental problem. Your best move is to talk with your child's pediatrician about your child's toilet-training history and current behavior and, if requested, take him in for a checkup. If there are no physical problems, your concerns will be put to rest. If there is a developmental delay or physical issue, your prompt attention will speed up the treatment process.

**Q:**   My daughter, now three, is fully trained, but she seems to hold it in until the very last minute, so we have to rush her to the bathroom before she has an accident. How can I get her to tell me sooner when she needs to go?

**A:**   Your child may not yet realize that she needs to use the bathroom until a minute or so before the need becomes too urgent to control. To help her increase her awareness of this need, when you notice her doing the "bathroom dance"—squirming or twisting in place or holding herself between her legs—say to her, "It looks like you need to use the potty," and casually suggest that the two of you "try and see." Set her on the potty (unless she resists strongly) and let her experience urinating in response to these actions. Creating a long lead-in time is usually simply a matter of teaching your child to link physical sensations with desired behavior.

**Q:**    **When my son goes to the bathroom he often has hard poops and has to take medicine to help soften it. What types of foods should I be giving him to help with this?**

**A:**    To help soften your child's stools, make sure he is eating foods high in fiber. Your child should eat plenty of fresh fruits, vegetables, and whole grains. Also, it's very important to make sure he is drinking plenty of water throughout the day.

## CHAPTER 7

# TOILET-TRAINING CHILDREN WITH SPECIAL NEEDS

The issue of when and how to begin toilet training can be more challenging for parents of children with special needs. The sense of accomplishment experienced when he does succeed in this important aspect of self-care can make an enormous difference in his level of self-esteem.

Perhaps more than other parents, those who have children with physical, mental, or developmental disabilities can appreciate the toilet-training process as a way to follow and celebrate a child's overall growth. Rather than focusing negatively on setbacks, which are inevitable for most children, they can use the setbacks as opportunities to discover how their child learns best and to demonstrate to him that he is able to progress.

## Signs of Readiness

Toilet training works best when parents of children with special needs have access to the guidance, instruction, and

encouragement of their pediatrician, other trained profes-
sionals including school personnel, support groups, or a
combination of all three. The first step a parent can take is to
determine whether the child is ready to begin. Signs of readiness are the same for all children:

- Is your child aware of the difference between being
  wet and being dry?
- Can he stay dry for at least two hours at a time?
- Can he sense when he needs to urinate or have a
  bowel movement, and is he capable of reaching the
  toilet or potty in time (perhaps with your help)?
- Can he undress and dress himself, or is he ready to
  learn?
- Is he motivated at some level to take this next step? If
  your child is in a resistant phase, is not ready to take
  on a new challenge, or does not yet feel the urge to
  behave "like other kids" in this way, you might take
  some extra time to prepare him mentally before
  starting the training process.

If you feel that your child is ready, ask your pediatrician
for her opinion. She can examine your child to offer a physical assessment and perhaps provide special insight into the
particular needs of your child. She can also give you further
information that you may need before starting, and let you
know what types of special equipment may be advisable.

It is important to prepare yourself emotionally before you
and your child begin the process. Children with special needs
often begin toilet training later than other children, frequently
completing the process at age five or even later. Of course,
children with some conditions may always need help with

their clothing (buttons, zippers, tights), and some might need help getting to the bathroom. Some will develop innovative ways of achieving independence.

Learning to use the toilet can be physically painful to some, initially incomprehensible to others. Accidents will happen, of course, and you will need to draw on an extra dose of patience and humor when they occur. Make sure that you obtain help from your spouse, relatives, or friends before you begin since it will be a journey much like other developmental achievements for your child.

## Physical Challenges

A number of physical disabilities and illnesses can hinder a child's ability to become fully toilet-trained or easily adjust to bathroom use. If your child faces such a situation, you should think about how your child's unique situation affects each stage of toilet training. Whether your child is unable to sense the need to urinate, has difficulty getting onto or staying on a standard potty or toilet, or must adjust or readjust to toilet use after having used an ostomy device, she will need extra support from you and her other caregivers as she learns to master this new skill.

### Visual Disabilities

Children with visual disabilities and those with sight deficiencies experience a disadvantage at several stages of toilet training. First, they might be unable to observe family members and peers using the toilet, so they cannot mimic their behavior. Many details of toilet or potty use—such as where the potty is in the bathroom, how the body is oriented to it as one sits down, how urine and poop get into the potty, or how one tears off and uses toilet paper—are simple to understand if a child can visually observe the process but may be difficult to comprehend if she cannot. Without sight to help her, your child will need to rely more on language to understand how the process works. Therefore, you will probably want to wait a little longer to begin the process—until she is three or four years old—so that she can fully comprehend what you are telling her.

## A PARENT'S STORY

### "What's Happening to Her?"

"My daughter, Elena, had a hard time with toilet training. We didn't start trying until she was four, and even then she couldn't seem to get the hang of it. After two months she was still having two or three accidents a day and she wet the bed nearly every night. I started to get really worried, but I'm glad I resisted the temptation to criticize Elena or blame her for failing to get to the bathroom. When I took her to the pediatrician, we learned that she has diabetes. Her need to use the bathroom frequently and her many accidents were symptoms of the disease.

"Now that we know she has diabetes, her progress in learning to stay dry has become a way to mark her adjustment to her new routine. Those days when she gets to the potty consistently are great morale boosters, helping build her confidence in the face of a difficult disease."

Angela, mother of Elena

When you are ready to introduce your child with a visual impairment to the concept of toilet use, start bringing her with you when you use the bathroom. Allow her to explore the bathroom and locate the toilet. (Be sure it is well ventilated and smells pleasant so she will want to return.) Place her hands on your shoulders so she can feel you sitting on the toilet, explain what you are doing and why, and guide her hands to the toilet paper dispenser. Also show your child the flush handle and the sink for hand washing.

Once you have placed a potty in the bathroom, lead her to it, let her accustom herself to its presence, and keep it in the

Children who are deaf and already fluent in sign language can rely on visual observation along with your explanations to understand the toilet-training process.

same place throughout the toilet-training process. Talk to her about toilet use at other times, too—pointing out that others use the toilet and that toilet use is a sign of being a big kid who can take care of herself.

Once your child begins practicing potty use herself, you will need to keep the bathroom and the path to it clear of obstacles. A musical potty that is activated when urine hits the bowl might make the learning process more fun. Teach her to feel the inner edge of the seat before tossing in the toilet paper. If the child is a boy urinating standing up at a toilet, show him how to position his body so he doesn't urinate on the toilet itself. (You may want to have your son initially sit to urinate; once he has mastered that skill, then you can teach him to stand in front of the toilet to urinate.)

Finally, as she grows more comfortable with bathroom use, make a point of taking her to the bathroom at each public place you visit. By helping her familiarize herself with the wide variety of bathroom layouts and toilet styles, you will help build her self-confidence when away from home and prevent accidents. And don't forget to reward her progress with praise, hugs, or small rewards.

## Hearing Disabilities

Children who have difficulty hearing or are deaf may or may not find toilet training challenging, depending on their ability to communicate. A child who is already fluent in sign language can rely on a combination of visual observation and explanations from you to understand what's expected of her, much like any other child. Children who do not yet have the ability to understand your signals and simple signs may not be ready for toilet training until they are somewhat older.

The key to training in these cases is to keep the process simple. When introducing the concept, emphasize the visual: allow your child to observe you (and, even better, other children) using the bathroom, and show her picture books about it. Choose one gesture or sign for each of the essential terms (*pee, poop, potty, wet, dry,* and *need to go*). Use these gestures each time you use the bathroom, and use them with her as well—signing "wet" (with a sad face) when you change her diaper or wet underwear, "dry" (with a happy expression) once she's been changed, and "need to go" after lunch when it's time to sit on the potty.

As long as you are consistent and stick with the half-dozen signals you need, your child will get the hang of potty use without longer explanations. When she does, be sure to reward her with plenty of hugs, or stickers she can put on a potty chart.

## Continence Problems

Some conditions have no effect on a child's ability to understand the process of toilet training but make it difficult for a child to comply. Your child may grow increasingly frustrated in her efforts to stay dry and may even give up trying.

The best solution to this dilemma is to put your child on a regular potty schedule. By placing her on the potty frequently (every one and a half to two hours or so), you remove the burden of having to acknowledge so many times each day that she must interrupt an activity to tend to her physical needs. Going to the bathroom at set times can become a habit similar to brushing her teeth twice a day or getting dressed in the morning, freeing her up to focus on other activities between visits.

# "PEOPLE ARE DIFFERENT": HOW TO TALK WITH YOUR CHILD ABOUT BATHROOM USE

As children approach preschool age, they become increasingly aware of the differences among people and are especially fascinated by any unusual behavior in their peers. Your three- to five-year-old is likely to become quite curious about the ways in which her bathroom use differs from that of other children and may encounter many questions and comments from her friends. Just as you have addressed differences in other areas of your child's life, it is important to provide her with positive statements and attitudes about her way of using the potty.

Start even before you begin training—emphasizing that the special new potty in the bathroom is hers alone and talking about how wonderful it will be for her to be able to take care of her bathroom needs herself, just like other kids. Create some standard responses for her to give to the questions she will probably get from playmates. Focus (and encourage her to focus) on her strengths rather than her disabilities.

Finally, encourage your child to be as self-sufficient as possible in her bathroom use. If she can learn to handle her own clothing and get to the bathroom with relative ease, she will feel like "one of the team"—and her attitude will convince others that she's right.

### Cerebral Palsy

Some children with cerebral palsy not only tend to be slow in developing bladder control but also may not have enough bladder awareness to begin toilet training at age two or three. If your child has cerebral palsy, she will need to be helped to develop an awareness that she needs to go (which may be signaled to you when you see her clutching her genitals or fidgeting anxiously). Take time to explain to her that when her body feels this way it means she has to go to the potty.

Your child will have to be able to delay urination until she is in position on the potty. She will need to remove her clothing and then hold herself on the potty (with supports, as described below) long enough to achieve success. Sometimes these challenges can be hard and may mean it is best to wait to toilet-train until she is older.

It is possible that limited physical activity, poor muscle tone, or medications could also cause constipation for your child with cerebral palsy, so pay special attention to her diet as you initiate the toilet-training process. Be sure that she is drinking plenty of fluids and eating foods high in fiber such as fresh fruits and vegetables. As she begins to practice removing her clothes before getting onto the potty, make it easier by providing clothes with Velcro fasteners or loose elastic waistbands. (She may find it easier to remove her clothes while lying down.)

### Spina Bifida and Spinal Cord Injury

Spina bifida, spinal cord injury, or spinal tumors create toilet-training problems for young children similar to those of cerebral palsy, but since most children with these conditions never develop an awareness of when they need to go, few can ever fully use a toilet. You can, however, teach your child to remove urine through a catheter on a regular basis, and to visit the bathroom for bowel movements on a regular schedule. A high-fiber diet with plenty of liquids and meals served on a regular schedule will make this process easier. Sometimes a stool softener or even a suppository or

Since most children with spina bifida and other spinal cord injuries never develop an awareness of when they need to use the toilet, you can teach your child to remove urine through a catheter and to visit the bathroom for bowel movements on a regular basis. Often this starts when a child is older, around six to eight years of age.

enema is required. Contact your pediatrician to discuss your child's needs. Since your child will find it difficult to remove her clothing, be sure to provide her with Velcrofastened clothes and allow her to lie down to undress if necessary.

A child with spinal cord dysfunctions will likely also not feel the need to move his bowels and will have a greater risk of developing constipation. He will need to be on a bowel regimen that is designed so that he has a bowel movement at home and then does not have a bowel movement at school. You will need to monitor him closely to keep him from becoming constipated by giving him adequate fluids, a diet high in fiber, and maybe a stool softener. Your pediatrician and therapist should be able to help develop a successful program for your child. He needs regular catheterizations, and either an aide or school nurse will have to help with the catheterizations until he is able to perform them himself.

## IS IT A SIDE EFFECT?

### Toilet Training and Medication

Whatever challenge your child with special needs faces, it is important to consider how toilet training is affected by medications. Depending on what medication she is taking, she may experience constipation, diarrhea, increased urine output, painful urination, or other side effects. If your child is taking medicine for her condition, talk with her pediatrician about its effects on elimination and how you can compensate for them.

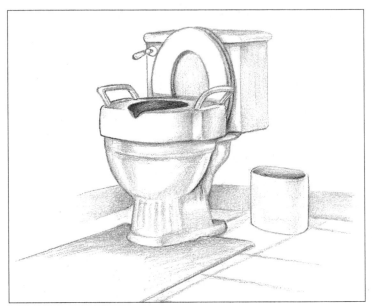

A special adapter seat placed on an adult toilet is best for children in wheelchairs, making it easier for them to use the toilet independently.

Parents of children with physical disabilities such as cerebral palsy or spina bifida may become so distracted by the need for special equipment or physical support that they forget about the necessary cognitive and emotional input that all children need to succeed at toilet training. The moment of installing that special potty in the bathroom is a good time to talk to your child about bathroom use and why it's important, to let her observe you and others using the bathroom, and to praise and reward her when she succeeds even a little bit. It is generally better to resist the temptation to "let things go" when there is some difficulty, and to remain firm about the schedule or routine you have created—unless the experience becomes negative and your child becomes very resistant. Remember, her progress in this arena is especially significant if it increases her self-confidence and prepares her for more challenges. Give her all the information, attention, and support she needs to succeed.

## Behavioral and Mental Disorders

Your experience toilet-training a toddler who has been identified as having developmental or behavioral difficulties will depend a great deal on your particular child's temperament, behavior patterns, and coexisting conditions. In this arena more than any other, perhaps, a parent's knowledge of a child's strengths, weaknesses, tendencies, and interests will help her through the process as much as any general guide.

Toilet training can be particularly trying for parents of children who have developmental disorders or behavioral difficulties—including those with autism spectrum disorder (ASD), fetal alcohol syndrome (FAS), oppositional defiant disorder (ODD), and, in cases when it is diagnosed this early, attention deficit/hyperactivity disorder (ADHD). Many children with these conditions may not be strongly motivated, or sufficiently equipped, to respond to the social reinforcements that work with other children (e.g., "What a big boy!"). For some, tangible rewards such as a sticker or a small toy can be effective. Many find it extremely difficult to adjust to any change in routine. Some are particularly sensitive to touch and other sensory inputs and become upset by the frequent pulling off and on of clothing, the physical closeness with an adult, and the unfamiliar surroundings of the bathroom.

For some children, simply learning the abstract concept of potty use can be complicated. For example, some children with behavioral disorders do not naturally imitate their parents' or peers' behavior. Others learn only through simple imitation or other concrete, nonverbal demonstrations. Such complications in the training process mean that early efforts can create a high level of frustration in your child and may lead to displays of temper, stubbornness, and refusal to cooperate.

Despite challenges, most children with special needs— whether they have physical challenges or behavioral issues— can be toilet-trained, though in some cases the learning process may take up to a year or even longer and require help from an occupational or physical therapist or a rehabilitation engineer. Your first step is to determine whether your child is ready to start training. Usually the time to think about beginning is when you notice that your child can stay dry for an hour or more at a time, has regular bowel movements, is aware that he is about to urinate or defecate, and dislikes being wet or soiled. It is also important to have your child examined by his pediatrician, since he may be at a higher risk for constipation or loose stools, which may interfere with training.

Once you have decided to begin, observe your child and consider carefully the specific traits, patterns of behavior, and obstacles that may impact his learning process. If he seems to dislike entering the bathroom, determine what the cause of his discomfort is—for example, the smell of disinfectant, the cold floor, or the sound of a flushing toilet—and change or neutralize it if possible (e.g., change cleansers, put socks on his feet, or move his potty away from the noisy toilet).

If he does not overtly signal the need to pee or poop, does he pause just before he has to pee or otherwise behave in a way that will provide you with a clue? At what times, or how long after eating or drinking, does he usually pee or poop? What foods, toys, or other objects is he most passionate about? These can be used as tangible potty-training rewards, which may prove more effective than praise.

Identify how your child learns best. Some respond to a firm but gentle physical demonstrations (being placed on the potty at regular times). Others do best with a formal routine containing a series of simple and predictable steps (verbally explained and reexplained, illustrated with pictures, or listed on a chart). Still others do best with offhand comments and conversations that inform without inviting resistance.

## Intellectual Disabilities and Developmental Disorders

Most children with developmental delay (DD), intellectual disability (ID), or an autism spectrum disorder (ASD) can be toilet-trained. The time it takes to achieve success ranges from a few months to a year or more. The process becomes easier as your child develops functional use of language, is able to manage his clothes (perhaps with some help from you), and shows awareness of the need to go.

Toilet training for children with DD, ID, or ASD can be quite similar to training for other children, but sometimes it is not. Like with other children, as you introduce your child to the concept of potty use, it often helps to keep explanations simple. Start by checking the state of his diaper or pants every hour or so and offering a one-word, nonjudgmental comment when he is wet ("Wet!"). After you change the diaper, smile and say "Dry!" If his verbal language skills are limited, you might substitute a special gesture, picture, or sign for the words *wet, dry, potty, need to go,* and so on.

Begin bringing him to the bathroom with you when you need to use it. After you've finished and pulled his pants up, smile and say "Dry!" If at all possible, have your child observe

## THE PROPER EQUIPMENT:
## AIDS TO HELP YOUR CHILD SUCCEED

A wide variety of toileting aids is now available for children with special needs. An occupational therapist who works with children with the same special needs as your child can often be a good resource for this adaptive equipment.

- **Clothing.** One of the simplest ways to ease the transition to bathroom use, as mentioned previously, is to provide clothing that is easy to remove and put on. Velcro closings, elastic waistbands, and front zippers are all simpler to manage than buttons, snaps, or fastenings in the back. Some parents allow their child to wear only underwear during the initial toilet-training period so that clothes do not become a hindrance.

- **Potties.** A number of potty designs will support your child and hold him in the proper position. They may be adjustable for height and provide special armrests, footrests, high or low back supports, a front bar to hold your child in place, splash guards, and casters with brakes. Most can be used in the shower as well, and some fit over adult toilets. Portable potties are also available that fold flat and provide armrests and a padded backrest. Wedge-shaped potties, which slide like a bedpan under your child's buttocks and back, work best for children who cannot sit up. Regular potties can also be modified at home in some instances, allowing you to provide extra support for your child at less cost.

- **Toilet adapter seats.** Special child-size toilet seats can be added to adult toilets as well. Lift seats help the child rise from a seated position on a toilet, using either springs, which require some arm strength to use, or a powered mechanism that lifts the seat up and forward. (Handrails attached to the wall will also help your child lift herself.) Padded seats, dish-shaped seats with a higher back and raised sides, armrests, and backrests offer greater stability while the child is sitting on the toilet. Seats that are slightly raised at the front will hold your child's legs apart, and a horseshoe-shaped seat, cut out at the front, may allow him to clean himself. Bottom wipers and tissue aids are available for children with limited arm mobility or restricted reach.
- **Wheelchair access.** For children in wheelchairs, access to the toilet can often be a tricky issue. The bathroom door must be wide enough for a wheelchair to fit inside. An adult toilet with an adapter seat is best for such a child, since the transfer from wheelchair to seat is fairly level. It is best if the wheelchair can enter the bathroom and line up beside the toilet without having to turn

around. Wall-hung toilets, with no supporting structures or outlet pipe at the base, make it easier for your child to position her wheelchair properly. Some of these toilets include padded seats, remote controls, and washing and drying mechanisms that are activated by seat contact. Many of these features can also be added to standard toilets. Whatever type of toilet you use, the seat should be between

other children using the bathroom, too. He may make the connection between himself and another child more easily than between himself and you. After you've finished and are dressed, show him how happy you are and tell him "Dry!" If he has a favorite doll or stuffed animal, use it to play potty, demonstrating again how the potty is used.

When he is ready to begin using the potty, begin setting him on it at regular times—quite frequently at first (as frequently as you checked him for wetness earlier) and then gradually settling down to the times when he usually goes. Try to keep him on the potty for five or ten minutes at a time—keeping him company, reading to him, playing tapes of children's music, and otherwise ensuring that he stays in place long enough to succeed.

Once he does pee into the potty, give him a big smile and say "Pee!" (or whatever word you have chosen for this event). Help wipe him and then praise him with a happy "Dry!" and give him a reward. Eventually, with enough repetition, he will understand the connection.

If your child has an intellectual disability or develop-

fifteen and nineteen inches high, and the floor space around the toilet must be forty-eight by sixty-six inches.

Some wheelchairs can be equipped with their own potties, and this might be best for initiating training. The chair's seat cushion is removed to reveal a toilet seat underneath. The removable pot is placed on a shelf installed beneath the seat.

mental delay, it is best to toilet-train him one step at a time. Don't expect your child to learn to signal or announce his need to go, pull down his pants, use the potty, wipe his bottom, and wash his hands as quickly as his typical peers might. Toilet training will work best if you focus on the actual act of elimination first and address the other skills later. It is more important to keep him motivated than to achieve instant success.

## Better Each Day

There is no doubt that toilet-training your child with special needs is a long-term challenge. But, even more than for other children, the rewards are enormous. Not only will your child exult in her new ability to care for herself in this important way—and not only will your own daily routine become simpler as a result—but many more opportunities may become open to your child as she grows older. A child with special needs who is toilet-trained is more likely to be accepted to, or promoted within, a preschool or childcare cen-

## SUCCESSES AND CONQUERING RESISTANCE

Once you have made the necessary adjustments in your child's environment and your teaching style, it is time to start working toward his first success. Some parents like to begin the training process with actual potty use, putting their child on the potty at a likely time and rewarding him when he uses it. Others—particularly those with a child who resists entering the bathroom—may want to focus on preliminary steps first. They may start by rewarding the child for entering the bathroom, then for approaching the potty or toilet, then for sitting on it, and finally for using it. (Extreme resistance is further discussed on page 170 in the box "Extreme Resistance: Children with Oppositional Defiant Disorder.")

To make this process easier, and to avoid the physical closeness that your child may resist, consider letting him wear only his underwear at first, or even nothing below the waist. Handling clothing can be taught at the very end of the process,

ter. Certain schools or residential treatment centers will accept your child only if she is toilet-trained.

If your child can look forward to some form of independent life as an adult, bladder and bowel control are musts. Even aside from these direct benefits, the self-confidence your child reaps

once the bathroom routine has been accepted as part of his day.

Some children tend to be resistant to adopting this new habit. It's important to insist, however—firmly but matter-of-factly—that he try. When accidents occur, don't punish or criticize your child for making a mistake.

If your child has difficulties with language, be sure to stick to simple instructions, and consider using visual reinforcers. As he gradually gets better at using the potty—motivated for the most part, perhaps, by the prospect of a small but tangible reward—your child's love of routine will begin to work in your favor. He will expect to visit the bathroom at predictable times and may even become upset if this doesn't happen. Until then, you will need to remind yourself how difficult this major step forward is for him. You should also think about how to find support for yourself as you search for the patience you will need to succeed. Both you and your child are embarking on a difficult developmental task.

from her new ability to tend to her body is likely to express itself in many other aspects of her life. As she sees that she can achieve a goal, maintain a routine, and be in some ways like other children her age, she will be able to take her place in society with greater optimism and a brighter outlook overall.

## EXTREME RESISTANCE: CHILDREN WITH OPPOSITIONAL DEFIANT DISORDER

If your child has been particularly oppositional, the relatively rigid new routine that toilet training necessarily imposes might be the type of situation most likely to lead to a battle. You will probably need to tailor your training program specifically to your child's needs. It is possible that physical placement on the potty, frequent reminders to visit the bathroom, and other methods that involve imposing a routine on your child will not work for you, even when other families use them with great success. Working with your pediatrician, who may be able to refer you to a clinical psychologist or behavior specialist, might be helpful.

For more ideas on how to avoid resistance, review the discussion in Chapter 6 as well as the list of tips on page 172.

## Q & A

### Why Is This Happening?

**Q:**    I feel like I am constantly asking my son if he has to use the bathroom and he always insists he doesn't. But he continues to have daytime accidents. What should I do?

**A:**    Some children can get very distracted by what they are doing at the time to realize what is happening until it's too late. Your child may get frustrated by continuing to have accidents. The best solution to this dilemma is to put your child on a regular potty schedule every 1½ to 2 hours. This way you don't have to burden your child by constantly asking him if he has to go. Going to the bathroom at set times can become a habit and hopefully he will have some success.

**Q:**    My husband and I disagree on when to start the toilet-training process for our daughter. We know she is going to have challenges and I want to wait a few more months, but my husband thinks we should start the process today.

**A:**    Sometimes the learning process for children with special needs will take a longer time and may require help from an occupational or physical therapist or a rehabilitation engineer. Your first step is to try and determine whether your child is ready to start training. Usually the time to think about beginning is when your child can stay dry for an hour or more at a stretch, has regular bowel movements, is aware that he is about to pee or poop, and dislikes being wet or soiled.

## AVOIDING RESISTANCE

To help minimize the chances that your child will resist your efforts:

- **Don't make an issue of it.** Some children adjust best to toilet training when it's casually introduced as something interesting that they might like to attempt. Mention that some of his friends now use the potty, and ask him if he wants to try.
- **Give him choices.** Point out that some kids like to have a potty chart with spaces for stars or stickers, and some like to get a small reward. Ask him how he would like to be rewarded for his successes on the potty. Let him choose between using a potty or the toilet, between the upstairs and downstairs bathrooms, and between diapers, training pants, or underwear at night.
- **Let him do the rewarding.** Your child may respond well to a chart that he can check off himself, or he may prefer using a grab bag of small treats from which he can choose after using the potty correctly.
- **Promote self-awareness.** Encourage your child to start noting on his own when he needs to use the bathroom, while you privately observe as well.
- **Offer your assistance.** Ask him if he wants you to lead him to the toilet, verbally remind

him, or give him a signal (clapping hands, ringing a bell) at the right times.

- **Avoid confrontations.** If he clearly needs to use the potty but refuses to go, don't argue, threaten, or otherwise give him a response he can react to. Try an offhand remark about how an accident will ruin today's record, or say, "Well, I need to go to the bathroom," and lead by example. If he has a tantrum, change the subject or walk away until he's calmer.

- **Take a breather if necessary.** If your child's resistance escalates beyond your ability to cope, drop toilet training for a while until it fades as an issue. Don't talk about it afterward or criticize him for his "failure." Rest assured that he will think about what happened and will bring the subject up when he's ready. When he does, follow his lead.

- **Praise and admire.** Your child may not show it, but he's keenly aware of your approval and appreciates it. Give him plenty of praise for every little success, and don't forget the hugs and kisses.

- **Let him learn from experience.** If he has an accident, point out calmly that he's wet now and enlist his help (in a pleasant, inviting way) in cleaning up. If he does help—or does anything at all positive—focus on this achievement rather than the accident.

## CHAPTER 8

## BEDWETTING

Four-year-old Eva's parents, Lisa and Bob, had not found toilet training easy a year ago. Their frequent disagreements over which routines and reinforcements worked best for Eva made the process more difficult than it should have been, and the disagreements slowed Eva's progress. It was a relief to both of them when Eva became reliably dry during the daytime and there was no more cause for argument.

But now, as Eva approached her fifth birthday, Bob's anxiety began to increase again. He pointed out to Lisa that Eva was still wetting the bed two or three times most weeks. None of Eva's friends' parents reported having this problem. He felt that Lisa's relaxed attitude—especially her willingness to put Eva in training pants at night—was the major reason behind what he called his daughter's "laziness." He insisted, increasingly loudly as Eva grew older, that she wear underwear at night, change her own sheets when she wet the bed, and go without dessert on the days following nighttime accidents.

Bob's response to Eva's experience sprang from a real concern over whether she was functioning normally and exercising the self-discipline appropriate for her age. Yet his uneasiness was based on a number of common misunderstandings about the causes of bedwetting, its frequency among four-year-olds, and implications regarding self-discipline. Bob did not realize, for example, that while most children become fully toilet-trained during the daytime between ages two and four, a large number are unable to stay dry through the night until age five or even older. There are perfectly understandable reasons for this.

Bob and Lisa's assumption that none of Eva's friends had a problem with bedwetting was probably also untrue. Parents of four- and five-year-olds can be much less forthcoming about their child's bedwetting incidents than they probably were about the travails of toddler potty training. Chances are good that many, if not most, of Eva's friends wet the bed now and then, but their parents did not perceive it as a problem or they wanted to avoid embarrassing their children. Because bedwetting continues to carry something of a stigma for many people, parents may be unaware of other children's experience and assume that their child is the only one with a problem.

Another common misconception about bedwetting at around age four or five is that it is somehow a moral issue having to do with self-discipline and respect for oneself and for others. In most cases the accidents occur without a child's awareness and ability to consciously control it. It is not a moral transgression that requires stern punishment. Even in cases when a young child is able to wake up and go to the bathroom but declines to do so, her reluctance is most likely a case of age-appropriate shortsightedness or fearfulness, not a sign of laziness.

## WHY DO YOUNG CHILDREN WET THE BED?

Some of the most common causes of bedwetting in young children include:

- **Typical development.** In most cases, children are delayed in developing the ability to stay dry through the night.
- **Family history.** Bedwetting runs in families. The rate triples if one parent has a history of wetting the bed as a child and increases five times if both parents have a history of wetting the bed.
- **Constipation.** If your child is constipated and has a lot of poop in the rectum, it can push against the bladder. This can cause him to have either nighttime wetting or daytime wetting. Keep a bathroom log to see how often your child poops.
- **Stress.** Bedwetting can be a response to changes or stresses at home, such as a new baby, moving, or divorce, or to stresses at school, such as difficulty adjusting to a new setting, academic pressure, or social pressure.

# DO OTHER KIDS WET THE BED?

A large percentage of children under age five experience bedwetting. It happens so commonly in young children because the nerves that control the bladder-brain connection are still maturing. After age five, the number of children who wet at night starts to decrease. About 15 percent of five-year-olds, 5 percent of ten-year-olds, and 1 percent of eighteen-year-olds experience occasional bedwetting. Such accidents are twice as common among boys as girls, and bedwetting occurs more often than daytime accidents.

Avoid making an issue of nighttime accidents. Instead, offer your child support and reassurance. You can also encourage her to help you change the sheets and clean up afterward.

## ASK YOURSELF

### Why Is Bedwetting So Upsetting?

Some adults may recall hurtful comments made about wetting the bed when they were children. It is important to understand that we now know, unlike our parents twenty or thirty years ago, how painful and even damaging remarks such as "This is disgusting. Get out of those pajamas" or "What were you thinking? How could you do this?" can be to a sleepy, confused child. Negative messages can increase a general sense of shame and lower a child's self-esteem.

If you find that you are frequently more angry, disgusted, or resentful over bedwetting than the situation really warrants, it may help to think about what your own experience was with this issue. How did your parents deal with bedwetting? How did they try to night-train you? Did nighttime accidents result in punishment, humiliation, or anger from parents and teasing from siblings?

If you feel that your experiences prevent you from responding more rationally, consider removing yourself from the scene and asking your spouse or partner to take charge of this issue. You can also teach your child to change her own pajamas and lay a towel over the sheets until morning, or encourage her to wear training pants until it's easier for her to stay dry.

## Bedwetting at Any Age: What to Look For

Completely successful nighttime toilet training is rare under age three; it is somewhat more common at ages four and five, but may not be achieved in many cases until a child is well into elementary school. Even later in life, particularly at times of stress, nighttime accidents happen. Still, there are times when bedwetting is not just part of everyday life but a symptom that needs attention.

If a child of any age has been completely toilet-trained for six months or longer and suddenly begins wetting the bed again, his parents should talk to his pediatrician. The sudden onset of bedwetting may signal a medical problem such as a bladder or kidney infection, diabetes, constipation, or defects in a child's urinary system (see Chapter 6). While less than

## RESPONDING TO BEDWETTING AT NIGHT

While bedwetting is commonly due to a delay in full-bladder awareness, something that is not always within a child's conscious control, it is best to reduce the actual impact of the wetting by offering training pants at bedtime or layering a sheet over a pad that lays over a second sheet and pad so you can simply peel off one layer should you need to prepare a dry bed in the middle of the night. Meanwhile, rest assured that bedwetting will decrease as your child's body matures. By the teen years, almost all children have outgrown the problem.

1 percent of bedwetting cases actually turn out to be related to diseases or defects, it is important to eliminate this possibility before moving on to other possible causes. In most cases when a disease or defect is the issue, other symptoms occur as well, including:

- Frequent urination during the day
- Discomfort or burning while urinating
- Unusual straining during urination
- Dribbling, daytime accidents, or a very small or narrow stream of urine
- Cloudy or pink urine, or bloodstains on his underpants or pajamas
- Daytime as well as nighttime wetting
- Leakage of stool into the underwear, or trouble controlling bowel movements

A sudden onset of bedwetting may also signal psychological stress, emotional problems, or physical or sexual abuse. If you suspect that any of these issues may be behind your child's bedwetting behavior, it is vital to share this information with your pediatrician. He will know what questions to ask your child to begin to explore these possibilities.

### Bedwetting after Age Five: Physical and Emotional Causes

A child who has not developed nighttime bladder control by age six and does not have a history of nighttime wetting in her family has a slightly increased chance of having a physical problem such as a narrowing of the bladder outlet or urethra, an overactive bladder, a small bladder capacity, or constipation.

If your child's bedwetting does not begin to diminish by age six, schedule an appointment with her pediatrician. Keep a list of your observations and share all the symptoms you have observed. Your doctor will ask you a number of questions aimed at identifying or eliminating any of a number of medical conditions, including some or all of the following:

- Is there a family history of bedwetting?
- How often does your child urinate and at what times of day?
- How often does your child have a bowel movement? Are the bowel movements large or hard? Does he strain to move his bowels? Is your child having any accidents with bowel movements?
- When does your child wet the bed? Is your child very active, upset, or under unusual stress when it happens?
- What type of beverages does your child drink throughout the day?
- Does your child tend to wet the bed after having carbonated beverages, citrus juices, or a lot of water in the evening or close to bedtime?
- Is there anything unusual about how your child urinates or the way the urine looks?
- Does your child snore at night or seem excessively tired during the day?

To answer these questions you may need to observe your child's bowel and bladder activities for a few days. Keep a log in the bathroom and share this information with your pediatrician.

Most children who wet the bed will gradually improve, with 15 percent becoming dry with each additional year of maturity without any specific intervention. Even in the case of physical problems or delays, most bedwetting diminishes naturally. Bladder control or capacity may increase, an overactive bladder may begin to settle and hold urine more efficiently. If your pediatrician decides that your child may have more significant problems, however, he may order additional tests such as an ultrasound of the kidneys or bladder. If necessary, he will recommend that your child see a pediatric urologist, who is specially trained to treat children's urinary problems. Your child will manage best with the support of experts in the field.

In some cases, you may find that your school-age child resumes bedwetting after having been dry longer than six months. If so, it is important to have her examined by her pediatrician. As discussed earlier in this chapter, a sudden resumption of bedwetting may signal a bladder or kidney infection, unrecognized constipation, or even diabetes, and merits immediate attention.

Emotional distress is another possible cause for a fresh series of bedwetting incidents. Many children wet the bed when they first begin to attend school. A move to a new house and the arrival of a new sibling are other common precipitants of nighttime accidents. Your child may be experiencing academic pressure or social conflicts, or she may be responding to stress in the family. Children who have experienced physical or sexual abuse also frequently revert to bedwetting. If you suspect anything, contact her pediatrician right away.

If you think that stress or any other emotional issue may be behind your child's accidents, talk with her about it. By helping her solve the problems that are causing her distress, you will not only support her emotionally but probably stop the bedwetting as well. If you find that she is not responding to your attempts to help her, consider getting professional help before her problems grow worse.

### Staying Dry at Night: Parenting Techniques, Tools, and Medications

Training a child to refrain from bedwetting differs fundamentally from daytime toilet training in that bedwetting is generally not under a child's conscious control. If your child can still sleep through nearly anything—not responding when you move him from one place to another or when making a lot of noise in his presence—he may also fail to respond to his body's nighttime signal that his bladder is full. If his bladder has not yet fully matured, it may overflow even if you wake him an extra time to use the potty before you go to bed. If he is experiencing a medical condition or emotional stumbling block, nighttime dryness will probably not occur until the underlying issue has been resolved.

For this reason, dealing with bedwetting is largely a matter of taking all possible practical steps to prevent nighttime accidents, keeping the cleanup process as painless as possible when it happens, and focusing on keeping your child's and your own spirits up while you wait for nature to take its course. Following are techniques that many parents have found to be helpful in supporting their children through this challenging period.

## SOCIAL CONCERNS: "WHAT IF I HAVE AN ACCIDENT?"

When your child was two or three, she was probably not particularly upset by her nighttime accidents. But as she grew older and entered elementary school, her increasing social awareness and desire to fit in with her peers may have led to feelings of discomfort, embarrassment, and even withdrawal as her bedwetting continued. If your school-age child is still struggling with issues relating to bladder control, it is important to consider her feelings as you discuss the problem with her, with family members, and with her pediatrician. When possible, let her decide whom she wants to know about this situation and allow her to describe it in her own way.

Ask her permission before divulging this information to someone new, and establish a no-teasing rule among siblings and friends. Run interference for her when she is invited to sleepovers, camping trips, or other overnight activities. (If she does not yet feel comfortable taking this risk, step forward and tell her friends, or their parents, that she has another commitment that weekend.) Most important, make sure that she understands that bedwetting is not her fault. In most cases, her nighttime accidents are a result of being physically unable to control her bladder. With patience and help, this situation will end.

- **Protect the bed and layer the linens.** Earlier in this chapter we suggested steps such as covering your child's bed with a waterproof mattress pad or absorbent bed mat, covering the pad with a sheet, and then adding another pad and another sheet. That way, if your child has an accident at four in the morning, it is only necessary to strip off the top sheet and pad before returning to bed.
- **Let your child help.** Encourage your child to help change the wet sheets and covers. This teaches responsibility. At the same time it can relieve your child of any embarrassment from having family members know every time he wets the bed. Be sure to avoid treating this as a punishment, however. Punishing your child for wetting the bed is likely to lead to resistance on his part, increasing rather than decreasing bedwetting behavior and making her more self-conscious.
- **Set a no-teasing rule in your family.** Do not let family members, especially siblings, tease your child for wetting the bed. Explain to them that their brother or sister does not wet the bed on purpose. If you refrain from making bedwetting an issue every time it occurs, other family members will follow.
- **Take steps before bedtime.** Have your child use the toilet right before bed.
- **Have your child avoid drinking large amounts of fluid for at least an hour before bedtime.** Encourage her to drink freely (especially water) throughout the day, so she will naturally be less thirsty in the evening. Avoid caffeinated drinks. Explain the purpose of drinking less before bed to your child so that he won't see it as a punishment.

- **Try to wake him up to use the toilet.** Before you go to bed wake your child and see if he can use the bathroom one more time.
- **Install a night-light in his room.** A light may help your child brave the scary journey to the bathroom at night.
- **Let him know you're there for him.** Tell your child explicitly that he's allowed to call to you in the middle of the night if he needs help getting to the bathroom.
- **Keep a potty nearby.** Potties don't have to be in the bathroom. Your child may be able to make it to the potty if it's only a foot or so from the bed.
- **Don't throw away the training pants.** Even if your child refuses training pants in the first flush of day-training success, he may have second thoughts later as the nighttime accidents pile up. Keep a supply of training pants on hand and give him a chance to change his mind without embarrassment.
- **Allow your child to choose.** If your child wants to try going without training pants and sleep in underwear, let her. Provide encouragement for her to "listen for her bladder" during the night.
- **Consider protecting the bed from wetness rather than the child.** An absorbent bed mat is an alternative to training pants in children over six, especially if your child feels embarrassed wearing what to him seems like a diaper. The knowledge that he is no longer wearing something to catch the urine may lead to more rapid recognition of wetness and waking.
- **Notice and praise the positive behaviors.** Praise will promote more dry nights, as it will encourage your

child to remember to use the toilet before bed, limit drinks in the evening, and help to change the bedding. All this allows your child to feel more in control of her body.

- **Reward him for dry nights.** Praise your child with stickers for his potty chart or other small rewards.

If you have followed all of these guidelines for one to three months and your child is still not able to stay dry during the night, your pediatrician may recommend using a bedwetting alarm, especially if your child is age seven or older. These alarms, which come in several types—wearable, wireless, and bell and pad—have a sensor that detects small amounts of moisture and turns on the alarm. This helps arouse your child and helps her brain realize that she has to go to the potty. Be sure your child resets the alarm before going back to sleep.

Many children will not wake up when the alarm goes off, so you will need to be prepared to wake your child as soon as possible after the bedwetting alarm goes off. You can put a baby monitor in her room to hear the alarm; some of the newer alarms have optional monitors that are meant to go in the parent's bedroom.

New types of alarms come out from time to time, so check with your pediatrician to see if there is a current model that will work better for you. Most pharmacies do not carry bedwetting alarms, or if they do, they don't stock the more effective ones. Bedwetting alarms can be purchased directly from the manufacturer and from resellers. They produce a 50 to 75 percent cure rate when used consistently and correctly, although some children occasionally relapse once they stop using them. Alarms tend to be most helpful when children wet enough for the conditioning to work. The bedwetting alarm, while the most effective treatment, also takes the most work, and so success requires both a motivated child and motivated parents. Successfully using an alarm system can be challenging, and 30 percent of children drop out of alarm treatment because they don't get the support they need when using the device.

If, after four to six months, the bedwetting alarm does not solve the problem, your pediatrician may prescribe an oral medication. Medication is usually a last resort and is not recommended for children under age six. Desmopressin is the most common medication used. About half of children are helped by this medication, which can provide some relief and

Have your child use the bathroom and avoid giving him large amounts of fluid before bedtime to help prevent nighttime accidents.

enable children to attend sleepovers or other overnight activities. Although they can be helpful for older children, all medications have side effects. Possible side effects of desmopressin include headaches, facial flushing, nausea, hyponatremia (low blood salt), and seizures. Your pediatrician will discuss the options with you, if necessary.

## "BUT DOES IT WORK?": AVOIDING UNPROVEN TREATMENTS

Because bedwetting is such a common problem, many mail-order treatment programs and devices advertise that they are the cure. Use caution, as many of these products make false claims and promises and may be expensive. Your pediatrician is the best source for advice, and you should ask for it before your child starts any treatment program.

Even after you have tried all of these methods for several months at a time, it is possible that your child will not respond to any treatment. This is not his fault—he probably wants to stop wetting the bed as much as you want him to!— and you can best support him by providing the reassurance he needs. As you wait for his body to mature to the point where bedwetting ends, try to focus more on other areas of his life in which he is clearly successful.

If you believe that some cause other than slow but normal physiological development is at work, talk again with your pediatrician or with a mental health professional. Otherwise, it is important for your child's self-confidence and emotional well-being for him to know you are proud of all of his accomplishments and that he is not defined by this single struggle.

# Q & A

## Why Is This Happening?

**Q:**    Does bedwetting run in families?

**A:**    Research has shown that bedwetting clearly runs in families. Fifteen percent of children without a history of bedwetting in their family will wet the bed. If one of the parents has a history of having wet the bed as a child, the rate goes up to 44 percent; it goes up to 77 percent if both parents had a history of it.

**Q:**    My eight-year-old daughter was born extremely premature. Could this have any bearing on why she still wets the bed?

**A:**    Continual bedwetting beyond age six can sometimes result from physiological, hormonal, or developmental problems. Since an extremely premature child is at greater risk for developmental difficulties, it is possible that her bedwetting is a result of her prematurity. However, it is somewhat more likely that she simply inherited her bedwetting tendency and would have experienced it whether or not she was born prematurely. It is important to have your child examined by her pediatrician to determine the cause of her continued bedwetting. In most cases, children grow out of this condition, even when it is inherited. However, it is always important to eliminate the possibility of any defects or delays when attempting to treat such a problem.

CHAPTER 9

# THE SELF-SUFFICIENT CHILD

If you are like most parents, you are delighted to see your child successfully concluding the toilet-training process. The days of loading the grocery cart with diapers are behind you (at least with this child), and accidents have dwindled to a manageable few.

But the completion of toilet training signifies much more than liberation from diapers. By learning to control this bodily function, your child has moved significantly closer toward self-mastery—every young child's goal. Responding to your wish for him to use the toilet "like a big boy" and practicing this new skill and succeeding again and again have given him a wonderful new sense of accomplishment and even independence. This feeling that he can successfully meet a challenge will add to his confidence in other areas of his life, including social and academic pursuits. Even in the face of occasional accidents, then, it is important to recognize the level of accomplishment your toilet-trained child has reached.

## WHAT IT HAS TAKEN TO
## BECOME TOILET-TRAINED

In learning to use the bathroom on his own without reminders, your child has had to learn the following skills:

- Recognize the need to go to the bathroom
- Compare his behavior to that of others
- Formulate a plan to get to the bathroom on time and carry it out
- Remember instructions and actions from one potty session to the next
- Remove his own clothing and put it back on
- Verbalize his need to go, along with any fears, anxieties, confusion, or resistance he may feel
- Overcome distractions and stay focused on going to the bathroom
- Wake up at night when he needs to go; get out of bed and go to the bathroom on his own
- Maintain these new habits even in unfamiliar environments and in stressful situations

Children change a great deal as they grow, but certain elements of their personality and learning style remain remarkably stable over time. Before you close the door on the toilet-training experience, take some notes on what you observed about your child's approach to learning and which of your training techniques worked best. You may be surprised at how easily you can transfer the lessons you have learned at this stage to other learning experiences later in his life.

### What Will You Learn About Yourself?

One of the fascinations of parenthood is that many of our own long-unexamined assumptions and buried emo-

Having mastered the skills of toilet use, your child will recognize the need, even in public places, to use the bathroom.

tions surface as we interact with our children. When your child was first born, you may have been surprised at how you responded to each new experience. You may have been awed or frightened by the act of childbirth, enchanted by or apprehensive about breastfeeding, confident or anxious the first time you held your child. Toilet training also evokes a wide range of feelings, from anxiety to frustration. Toilet training is a valuable task that every parent must undertake. But its greater value lies in its power to teach parents more about their children, themselves, and their lives together as a family. Ideally, in the years to come you will be able to draw on lessons learned during this task to communicate effectively, promote desirable behavior, approach new challenges in positive ways, and toilet-train future children with greater ease.

## What Will You Learn About Your Child?

The toilet-training process not only offers you new insights into your own emotions, attitudes, and parenting approach but also allows you a fascinating look at your child's personality and learning style. Once toilet training is more or less completed, think back on your child's experiences. Which parts of the process were easy for him and which were more difficult? Did he have a hard time sitting still on the potty for more than thirty seconds or so? Did he become so involved with other activities that he frequently forgot to go? Did he tend to mimic whatever child he was with at any given time—using the potty if the other child did, but having an accident if the other child was still in diapers?

An observant parent will notice how much more effective positive reinforcement is with children than criticism or pun-

# A PARENT'S STORY

## A Stitch in Time

"It wasn't until I potty-trained my second child, Emma, that I was able to make the connection between my own habits and my successful efforts to teach her things. With my first child, Richard, I was never prepared—I never remembered to pack extra clothes or diaper wipes or otherwise prepare for possible accidents. As a result, whenever Richard had an accident outside of the house (or even at home), I was likely to fall apart completely. These emotional outbursts of mine were really hard on both of us, and they didn't make the situation any better. Six years later, when potty-training Emma, I was an older parent who had learned to come prepared. I assembled all the necessary cleaning supplies before I even introduced her to the potty, and we never left the house without a change of clothes. I couldn't believe what a difference it made, not only in my general stress level but also in my relationship with Emma and her level of self-esteem.

"Since the potty-training period ended, I have found it so easy to teach her new things. She is such a confident little person and knows I won't blow up if she makes a mistake. It's hard to believe that so much good can come from remembering to pack a bag or put a plastic liner on the bed. Overall, I'd say that through potty training my kids taught me at least as many valuable lessons in self-management as I taught them."

Ellen, mother of Richard and Emma

ishment. The desire to please a parent and to be praised, loved, and rewarded is extremely powerful in most young children.

Toilet training is one of the best times to witness and appreciate this motivation in your child. As your child moves on to kindergarten and elementary school, your continued positive interest and rewards for progress will keep his desire to please alive, helping him achieve academic, social, and personal success.

## What Will You Learn About Your Family?

Some of the more frequent insights you will experience during the toilet-training process have to do with the ways in which your family works together. Chances are you notice over the six months or longer that toilet training generally

## TAKING NOTES

Which training techniques worked best—talking a great deal with him about potty use or simply placing him on the potty, sticking to a regular schedule or just letting him sense when he needed to go? Did he appreciate your reminders to go to the bathroom or did he perceive them as controlling and resist? Did he respond better to hugs and kisses, words of praise, stars on a chart, or promises of fun activities if he stayed dry through the day or the week?

## "HOW WOULD I DO IT DIFFERENTLY?"

Nobody's perfect, and nearly every parent carries around a mental list of things he would do differently if he had the chance to relive a particular experience with his child. Below is a list of common post-toilet-training resolutions that you may consider as you look forward to the years ahead.

- **"I'd identify my emotional triggers and back off when I experience them."** We all have emotional responses to certain situations. It's a fact that young children tend to inadvertently trigger our impatience as they struggle to learn proper behavior. When toilet-training your child, you may have noticed that you lost control of your emotions most easily when you hadn't had enough sleep, when you were caught unprepared, or when you were distracted by work. You probably recognize the signals that your anger is getting out of hand. By identifying these danger signs ahead of time, you can teach yourself to step back before you lose your temper and take a time-out, talk with another adult, or use another method to let off steam.

- **"I'd wait until I was alone with my partner before arguing about our parenting style."** Studies have shown that disagreement or conflict between parents over rule setting and enforcement techniques has a more negative long-term effect on children than the consistent use of even less-than-ideal practices (aside from physical, verbal, or emotional abuse, which must never be tolerated). If you strongly disagree with your partner's parenting style, work out a compromise in private, before another conflict occurs with your child, and then focus on consistently enforcing this new method. Partners who cannot agree with each other's basic philosophy of parenting should concentrate on specifics, agreeing ahead of time on what they will do when, say, their child refuses to go, or begs for sweets right before dinnertime. These partners should also consult their child's pediatrician.

- **"I'd worry less about the mess and focus more on my child's self-esteem."** Unexpected chaos is part of every family's life. You can always clean up after an accident. What's important is that your child understands that she is loved, valued, and supported.
- **"I'd try to maintain a sense of humor and remember that this too shall pass."** Parents are often surprised to look back on the toilet-training process and see that what felt like an endless series of challenges lasted for only a few months or so. It's a well-known fact that children grow up all too quickly. With a little effort, even difficult stages can be made fun and fascinating most of the time.

takes that you (or your partner) take on the role of family disciplinarian while your partner (or you) prefers a more permissive approach. (All references in this section to a partner can be applied to any other adult involved in raising your child.) Or you may notice that your child generally goes to one parent when she has an accident and to the other when she announces her success. You and your partner may also learn to recognize the signs indicating when one of you reaches his or her limit, requiring quick intervention from the other. Finally, you may notice that one of you may be more inclined to "do" for your child, while the other is more likely to help her to be as independent as possible—a pattern that may continue for years. The main thing to remember is that she will have separate relationships with both of her par-

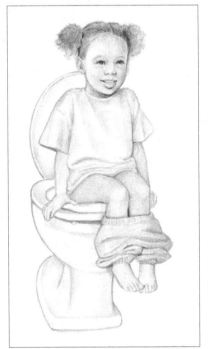

Through toilet training, your child has learned to accomplish goals, become confident and independent, and developed physical and emotional skills that will assist her throughout her life.

ents and that this is all part of growing up and becoming herself.

In the meantime, you can use what you observe about your patterns as a family to make whatever changes you think are necessary. Perhaps you will find that the two of you tend to "gang up" on your child when she makes a mistake, overwhelming her rather than allowing her room to understand and correct her mistake. Or you may notice that when you and your partner disagree over your approach to a parenting problem, you each tend to follow your own course, undermining the other's efforts instead of agreeing on a viable compromise. Reserve some time to discuss these issues alone with your partner or together with your child's pediatrician. You may even talk with your child on a simple level about which parenting techniques lead her to feel better or worse.

## Enjoying Your Self-Sufficient Child

When it comes time for your toilet-trained child to say good-bye to toddlerhood and move on, you can congratulate yourself on the completion of a major parenting challenge. Your child has become more confident and independent as a result of your efforts to help him achieve this developmental milestone, and his pride in his ability to master a new skill will support his further development.

The simple fact that he has experienced the pleasure of achieving a goal will make later success more likely. In the years to come, accidents will happen now and then. What's important is that your child and your family have accomplished something together and you are now better prepared to meet the challenges that lie ahead.

# INDEX

Page numbers of illustrations appear in italics.

## ABOUT THE AUTHOR

MARK WOLRAICH, M.D., F.A.A.P., is the Shauna Walters Professor of Pediatrics, Edith Kinney Gaylord Presidential Professor and Chief of the Section of Developmental and Behavioral Pediatrics at the University of Oklahoma Health Sciences Center. He has participated in and chaired a number of committees in the American Academy of Pediatrics and is past president of the Society for Developmental and Behavioral Pediatrics. He has been awarded the C. Anderson Aldrich from the AAP and the Salk Award from the Society for Pediatric Psychology and was inducted into the Children and Adults with ADHD Hall of Fame.

The AAP is an organization of 64,000 primary-care pediatricians, pediatric medical subspecialists, and pediatric surgical specialists dedicated to the health, safety, and well-being of all infants, children, adolescents, and young adults. This book is part of the ongoing educational efforts of the Academy to provide parents and caregivers with high-quality information on a broad spectrum of children's health issues. AAP books with Bantam include *Caring for Your Baby and Young Child: Birth to Age 5, Your Baby's First Year, Caring for Your School-Age Child Ages 5 to 12,* and *New Mother's Guide to Breastfeeding.*